LAMDA

ANTHOLOGY OF VER

LAMDA

ANTHOLOGY OF
VERSE AND PROSE
VOLUME XII

PUBLISHED BY
MAX REINHARDT
FOR THE LONDON ACADEMY OF MUSIC
AND DRAMATIC ART

British Library Cataloguing
in Publication Data
LAMDA anthology of verse and prose.
Vol. XII
1. Recitations   2. English literature
I. London Academy of Music and Dramatic Art
820.8   PRI 109

ISBN 0 370 31131 0
ISBN 0 370 31132 9 Pbk

Printed in Great Britain for
Max Reinhardt Ltd
32 Bedford Square, London WC1B 3EL by
Redwood Burn Ltd, Trowbridge, Wilts
Photoset by Rowland Phototypesetting Ltd
Bury St Edmunds, Suffolk
First published 1988

The Examination Syllabus can be obtained from:

Tower House
226 Cromwell Road
London   SW5 0SR

Principal of Examinations: Brian R. Tilston. L.L.A.M. (Hons)

CONTENTS

INTRODUCTION

There exists a recording of an interview with Walter de la Mare, made shortly before he died. Sitting in his room, he talks about this and that, feeding titbits to the tape-recorder in a rather wary and cornered way. Eventually, he deflects attention to a tree, visible from his window. He then goes on to recall how one day during a thunderstorm he happened to be watching that tree just as a bolt of lightning struck it. The bang and flash were startling enough, but not as startling as what the tree did. The tree, he said, simply threw off all its bark – 'Like a woman taking off her petticoat.'

His description of this, the slow musing phrases of his old but wonderfully alert and living voice, the surprised and surprising cadences of it, as that marvellous, shocking, curious moment rises again before him, make up one of the most uncanny vocal evocations I know.

What seals the purity of it is that his anecdote is followed, almost immediately, by his recitation of one of his poems. The effect is of a sudden closing-off. Not that he was a bad reader of his own verse. Rather the opposite. Listening to him there, you hear what you hope to hear from a poet's reading of his or her own verse: you hear the peculiar, inner music, the singing ensemble of psychological components, which determines the possibilities of the verse. And he does project the verse perfectly.

But you listen in vain for the de la Mare of the lightning-blasted tree. The delicate, searching, naked music with which he unearthed the memory of that vision, and in which you seemed to hear the inmost secret chords of his sensibility – that is absent.

For any of us who recite verse or prose there is a lesson here.

Another odd experience showed me a different lesson. I had made an adaptation of Seneca's *Oedipus*, for Peter Brook. Working towards the simplest, most direct release of the energies in that strange play, I had reduced the original to a skeletal oratorio and a vocabulary of a bare few hundred words. At the same time, I had tried to maintain, overall and in detail, a sense of pattern: patterns of rhythms, patterns of weight and of mood, patterns of cadences, just as in a piece of music. And the actors were of a quality that could make the most of this: they included Irene Worth, Sir John Gielgud, Colin Blakely, Ronald Pickup, all virtuoso speakers of verse and shapers of scenes.

Two or three days before the opening night, Peter Brook lined up the entire cast on stage (thirty-six altogether) and asked them to declaim the play, from where they stood, without moving a limb, at double speed, and in very loud, flat, Dalek-like voices – i.e., without any expressive inflection whatsoever. The purpose of this exercise was to shake them out of any constraining mannerisms that might have become fixed and mechanical during the very long rehearsal. But the results were unexpected.

The actors set off, full tilt. Within minutes, I realised I was undergoing a new, extraordinary verbal experience. The play, in fact, had become utterly verbal, in an unfamiliar but overpowering way. Without the visual distraction of actors acting, and without the cerebral distraction of voices interpreting, but at a speed which demanded the utmost concentration of attention, the words began to happen in a depth where their meanings were liberated and magnified. It was the reverse of supersonic: we were all packed inside a hurtling rocket that had shed every material circumstance and was now travelling on in pure sound. It is difficult to describe or to know just what was going on, but everybody felt it. The field of electrical power became nearly unbearable. One of the actors fainted, and a stage hand sitting in the front row also fainted. When it was over Peter Brook and I looked at each other in astonishment.

It occurred to me then: were Shakespeare's plays performed in something approaching this style, this speed and inwardness, this explosive, express containment? Was this how those colossal structures got airborne? And in fact, the closest thing to it that I have heard was the Comédie Française playing Racine and, indeed, *Richard III*.

I felt I had glimpsed a whole greater existence of drama, one which our English stage has forgotten. Maybe this was how the rigid, stilted, masked actors of the Greek amphitheatre performed their megaphone tragedies and sent members of their audience raving in iambics for days afterwards.

Those Greek plays were close to liturgy. The gods and the underworld were still listening, and it was intended that they should hear. And not only in Ancient Greece, but all over the world, in all places, at all times, wherever men try to reach the ear of spirits, or of gods, or of God, they use incantatory speech. They abandon all workaday tones and inflections – without which we human beings can hardly understand each other – and resort to this more or less frenzied plainsong. As if those spirits, etc., have somehow let it be known that they will listen to nothing else. And this is inborn. We all discover it the moment we need to pray.

We seem to have strayed some way from Walter de la Mare and his tale of the tree. But not so far, maybe, from Yeats's reading of his poems, or from Eliot's.

Whether we approve or not, we have to accept that when we recite verse or shaped prose we invoke something. And what hears us, and approaches, is human spirit: closer and fuller human spirit. The question is: what is human spirit, is it a desirable thing? And do we want a little, a medium amount or a lot? How deep is it? Where does it end? What powers swim up or fly down through it? Are they frightful or benign? And we have to think of the reciter too. Is the reciter looking for amusement, or a thrill or a scare? For what is he looking? And is he inside a magical, protective circle or out of it?

In his lecture on the Duende, Federico Garcia Lorca gives an account of what some people, at one time and in one place, expected of incantation. He describes the singing of the Andalusian flamenco singer Pastora Pavon in a tavern in Cadiz:

She sang with her voice of shadow, with her voice of liquid metal, with her moss-covered voice, and with her voice tangled in her long hair. She would soak her voice in manzanilla, or lose it in dark and distant thickets. Yet she failed completely: it was all to no purpose. The audience remained silent . . . Only a little man . . . said sarcastically in a very low voice, 'Viva Paris!' as if to say, 'Here we do not care for ability, technique or mastery. Here we care for something else.'

At that moment Pastora Pavon got up like a woman possessed, broken as a medieval mourner, drank without pause a large glass of cazalla, a fire-water brandy, and sat down to sing without voice, breathless, without subtlety, her throat burning, but – with Duende. She succeeded in getting rid of the scaffolding of the song, to make way for a furious and fiery Duende . . . that made those who were listening tear their clothes . . .

Something of the sort was described by Austen Henry Layard, in his memoir of the excavation of Nineveh. He tells there how an itinerant bard gave a performance, in the tent one night, to the tribesmen who were working on the dig, and how he, Layard, watched, in absolute incredulity, as the audience writhed on the carpets, cried out in anguish, ground their teeth – while the bard sang his epic.

Are these excesses? Incantatory dialogue with the Duende, or with its relatives, occupies the inner gulf, on the brink of which L A M D A holds its examinations. Few of us have much inclination to go over that brink. Walter de la Mare had no inclination to go over. And there he is on the brink, quite safe, with his tree. Teaching his exemplary lesson.

Or is he? Maybe what makes his tale of the tree so haunting is precisely that – a breath of the Duende. It doesn't disturb his teatime courtesy, but perhaps – it lifts the voice in those strange eddies. I vividly remember my response when I first heard Michael Hordern speak Shakespeare. I had come to believe it was impossible for a modern English voice and temperament to cope with that language convincingly. But there he was, speaking quite calmly, exactly as he speaks to his friends: a voice supercharged with intimate modulations, conscience, concern. And it was perfect. Those long speeches of Ulysses, in *Troilus and Cressida*, rose up and searched through all their complexities, very much as Walter de la Mare's voice searched through his memory of the lightning-struck tree. And just as naturally. Words and cadences clasping each other gently, naked, seemingly artless, inevitable, saturated with unforced emotion, enclosed in a deep, still imagination of the business in hand. Was the Duende there? Not the blood-freezing Duende of Pastora Pavon, maybe, but something – an overshadowing presence, an awareness. Not the speech of the Duende, but a darkness, a gulf, beneath the voice of the actor, in which the Duende listens.

Yet this is the delight of reciting verse and measured prose. It would be nothing if it were not walking a tightrope over such possibilities.

Ted Hughes
Poet Laureate

UNDERSEA

Beneath the waters
Green and cool
The Mermaids keep
A swimming school.

The oysters trot;
The lobsters prance;
The dolphins come
To join the dance.

But the jellyfish,
Who are rather small
Can't seem to learn
The steps at all.

Marchette Chute

LATE FOR BREAKFAST

Who is it hides my sandals when I'm trying to get dressed?
And takes away the hair brush that was lying on the chest?
I wanted to start breakfast before any of the others
But something's always missing or been borrowed by my
    brothers.
I think I'd better dress at night, and eat my breakfast too.
    Then when everybody's hurrying –
    I'll have nothing else to do.

Mary Dawson

FEET

Feet of snails
are only one
Birds grow two
to hop and run
Dogs and cats
and cows grow four
Ants and beetles
add two more
Spiders run around
on eight,
which may seem
a lot, but wait –
Centipedes
have more than *thirty*
feet to wash
when they get dirty

Aileen Fisher

WITCH, WITCH

'Witch, witch, where do you fly?' . . .
'Under the clouds and over the sky.'

'Witch, witch, what do you eat?' . . .
'Little black apples from Hurricane Street.'

'Witch, witch, what do you drink?' . . .
'Vinegar, blacking and good red ink.'

'Witch, witch, where do you sleep?' . . .
'Up in the clouds where pillows are cheap.'

Rose Fyleman

FIRST DAY AT SCHOOL

My first day at school today.
Funny sort of day.
Didn't seem to learn much.
Seemed all we did was play.
Then teacher wrote some letters
On a board all painted black.
And then we had a story and . . .
I don't think I'll go back.

Rod Hull

UNDER THE STAIRS

I don't like the cupboard
Under the stairs,
It reminds me of caves
And dragons' lairs.

So I never look in
Once it is night,
In case I should get
A nasty fright.

I'm silly I know
'Cos it's only small
There wouldn't be room
For a dragon, at all.

But even in daytime
It gives me the scares
To go past the cupboard
Under the stairs.

Daphne Lister

ROGER WAS A RAZOR FISH

Roger was a razor fish
as sharp as he could be.
He said to Calvin Catfish,
'I'll shave you
            for a fee.'
'No thanks,'
said Calvin Catfish,
'I like me like I be.'
And with his whiskers
on his face
he headed out to sea.

Al Pitman

SHOPPING

I'm going shopping with Mother,
She says it's going to be fun,
I know it's going to be boring,
Still she might buy me a bun,
She might buy a book or some
pencils,
Or something to cut out and stick,
But if she's just going to buy dresses –
I think I shall say I feel sick.

Mary Williams

———◆———

THE FLOWER-SELLER

The Flower-seller's fat, and she wears a big shawl!
She sits on the kerb with her basket and all;
The wares that she sells us are not very dear
And are always the loveliest things of the year.
        Daffodils in April,
          Purple flags in May,
       Sweet peas like butterflies
          Upon a summer day,
       Brown leaves in autumn,
          Green leaves in spring,
       And berries in the winter
          When the carol-singers sing.
The Flower-seller sits with her hands in her lap,
When she's not crying Roses, she's taking a nap;
Her bonnet is queer, and she calls you My dear,
And sells you the loveliest things of the year.

Eleanor Farjeon

GENERAL STORE

Someday I'm going to have a store
With a tinkly bell hung over the door,
With real glass cases and counters wide
And drawers all spilly with things inside.
There'll be a little of everything:
Bolts of calico; balls of string;
Jars of peppermint; tins of tea;
Pots and kettles and crockery;
Seeds in packets; scissors bright;
Bags of sugar, brown and white;
Biscuits and cheese for picnic lunches,
Bananas and rubber boots in bunches.
I'll fix the window and dust each shelf,

And take the money in all myself,
It will be my store and I will say:
'What can I do for you today?'

                              Rachel Field

THE SILVER ROAD

Last night I saw a Silver Road
Go straight across the sea,
And quick as I raced along the shore,
That quick road followed me.

It followed me all around the Bay,
Where small waves danced in tune,
And at the end of the Silver Road
There hung a Silver Moon.

A large round Moon on a pale green sky,
With a Pathway bright and broad;
Some night I shall bring that Silver Moon
Across that Silver Road.

                              Hamish Hendry

HELP!

Catch hold of my leg!
Catch hold of my toe!
I'm flying away
And I don't want to go.

I bought this balloon
Just a minute ago
From the man with a beard
Who's still standing below.

Why didn't he tell me,
Why didn't he say
A balloon of this size
Would just fly me away?

Catch hold of my leg!
Catch hold of my toe!
I'm flying away
And I don't want to go.

Barbara Ireson

BETWEEN BIRTHDAYS

My birthdays take so long to start.
They come along a year apart.
It's worse than waiting for a bus;
I fear I used to fret and fuss,
But now, when by impatience vexed
Between one birthday and the next,
I think of all that I have seen
That keeps on happening in between.
The songs I've heard, the things I've done,
Make my unbirthdays not so un-

Ogden Nash

THE WIND

I can get through a doorway without any key,
And strip the leaves from the great oak tree.

I can drive storm-clouds and shake tall towers,
Or steal through a garden and not wake the flowers.

Seas I can move and ships I can sink;
I can carry a house-top or the scent of a pink.

When I am angry I can rave and riot;
And when I am spent, I lie quiet as quiet.

James Reeves

ELETELEPHONY

Once there was an elephant,
Who tried to use the telephant —
No! No! I mean an elephone
Who tried to use the telephone —
(Dear me! I am not certain quite
That even now I've got it right.)

Howe'er it was, he got his trunk
Entangled in the telephunk;
The more he tried to get it free,
The louder buzzed the telephee —
(I fear I'd better drop the song
Of elephop and telephong!)

Laura E. Richards

THE DUSTMAN

Every Thursday morning
Before we're quite awake,
Without the slightest warning
The house begins to shake
    With a Biff! Bang!
    Biff! Bang! Biff!
It's the Dustman, who begins
    (*Bang! Crash!*)
To empty all the bins
Of their rubbish and their ash
    With a Biff! Bang!
    Biff! Bang! Bash!

Clive Sansom

AS FIT AS A FIDDLE

Grandfather George is as fit as a fiddle,
As fit as a fiddle right up from his middle,
Grandfather George is as fit as a fiddle,
As fit as a fiddle right down to his toes.

Grandfather George whenever I meet him
Nips my right ear and asks me a riddle,
And when Mother questions him how he is keeping,
He slaps his left leg and says 'Fit as a fiddle.'

Once I said 'Grandfather George, why a fiddle,
Why is a fiddle especially fit?'
He laughed very loud and said 'Hey diddle-diddle,
I'll give you a sixpence if you'll answer that.'

So now I ask everyone, friends and relations,
People I talk to wherever I go,
I ask them on buses, in shops and at stations:
I suppose, by the way, that you do not know?

Pauline Clarke

THE DESERTED HOUSE

There's no smoke in the chimney,
   And the rain beats on the floor;
There's no glass in the window,
   There's no wood in the door;
The heather grows behind the house,
   And the sand lies before.

No hand hath trained the ivy.
　　The walls are grey and bare;
The boats upon the sea sail by,
　　Nor ever tarry there.
No beast of the field comes nigh,
　　Nor any bird of the air.

Mary Coleridge

THE PUMPKIN

You may not believe it, for hardly could I:
I was cutting a pumpkin to put in a pie,
And on it was written in letters most plain
'You may hack me in slices, but I'll grow again.'

I seized it and sliced it and made no mistake
As, with dough rounded over it, I put it to bake;
But soon in the garden as I chanced to walk,
Why there was that pumpkin entire on his stalk!

Robert Graves

HE WHO OWNS THE WHISTLE, RULES THE WORLD

january wind and the sun
playing truant again.
Rain beginning to scratch
its fingernails across
the blackboard sky

in the playground
kids divebomb, corner
at silverstone or execute
traitors. Armed
with my Acme Thunderer
I step outside,

take a deep breath
and bring the world
to a standstill

Roger McGough

THE GERM

A mighty creature is the germ,
Though smaller than the pachyderm.
His customary dwelling place
Is deep within the human race.
His childish pride he often pleases
By giving people strange diseases.
Do you, my poppet, feel infirm?
You probably contain a germ.

Ogden Nash

I'M THE BIG SLEEPER

I'm the big sleeper
rolled up in his sheets
at the break of day

I'm a big sleeper living soft
in a hard kind of way

The light through the curtain
can't wake me
I'm under the blankets

you can't shake me
the pillow rustler
and blanket gambler
a mean tough eiderdown man

I keep my head
I stay in bed.

Michael Rosen

WINDY NIGHTS

Whenever the moon and stars are set,
   Whenever the wind is high,
All night long in the dark and wet,
   A man goes riding by.
Late in the night when the fires are out,
Why does he gallop and gallop about?

Whenever the trees are crying aloud,
   And ships are tossed at sea,
By, on the highway, low and loud,
   By at the gallop goes he.
By at the gallop he goes, and then
By he comes back at the gallop again.

Robert Louis Stevenson

THE NEW YEAR

From a surly
Night of winter
Moaning dourly
Over the snows,

I climbed early
New Year's morning
As the pearly
Frost-light rose,

And from a burly
Iron hilltop
Where the dreary
Jackdaws froze,

I saw clearly
Ploughlines where the
Summer barley
Always grows.

Ted Walker

CHAMELEON

I can think sharply
and I can change:
my colours cover a considerable range.

I can be some mud by
an estuary,
I can be a patch on the bark of a tree.

I can be green grass
or a little thin stone
– or if I really want to be left alone,

I can be a shadow . . .
What I am on your
multi-coloured bedspread, I am not quite sure.

Alan Brownjohn

WHO?

Who saw the smooth snow falling
All night long?
Who heard the white owl calling
Her strange, sad song?

Nobody.
Not anyone.
Not anyone at all.

Who heard the bleak wind howling
Over wild seas?
Who saw the starved fox prowling
Through ghostly trees?

Nobody.
Not anyone.
Not anyone at all.

Nobody saw winter walking,
Nobody heard winter talking.

Nobody.
Not anyone at all.

Leonard Clark

JOHN MOULDY

I spied John Mouldy in his cellar,
Deep down twenty steps of stone;
In the dusk he sat a-smiling,
  Smiling there alone.

He read no book, he snuffed no candle;
The rats ran in, the rats ran out;
And far and near, the drip of water
  Went whisp'ring about.

The dusk was still, with dew a-falling,
I saw the Dog-star bleak and grim,
I saw a slim brown rat of Norway
  Creep over him.

I spied John Mouldy in his cellar,
Deep down twenty steps of stone;
In the dusk he sat a-smiling,
  Smiling there alone.

Walter de la Mare

THE TOLL-GATE HOUSE

The toll-gate's gone, but still stands lone,
In the dip of the hill, the house of stone,
And over the roof in the branching pine
The great owl sits in the white moonshine.
An old man lives, and lonely, there,
His windows yet on the cross-roads stare,
And on Michaelmas night in all the years
A galloping far and faint he hears . . .
His casement open wide he flings
With 'Who goes there?' and a lantern swings . . .
But never more in the dim moonbeam
Than a cloak and a plume and the silver gleam
Of passing spurs in the night can he see,
For the toll-gate's gone and the road is free.

John Drinkwater

CHRISTMAS

For the sake of the angels who sang on high
Let not the birds lack food and die.
For the sake of the ox and ass in stall
Have mercy on dumb creatures all.

For the sake of Joseph the carpenter
To the poor and toiling be almoner.

For the sake of Mary, pure and low,
Tenderness to all women show.

For the sake of Christ, new come to birth,
Love every little child on earth.

And on thy head, like a diadem,
Shall rest the glory of Bethlehem.

Teresa Hooley

THE WITCHES' RIDE

Over the hills
Where the edge of light
Deepens and darkens
To ebony night,
Narrow hats high
Above yellow bead eyes,
The tatter-haired witches
Ride through the skies.
Over the seas
Where the flat fishes sleep
Wrapped in the slap of the slippery deep,
Over the peaks
Where the black trees are bare,
Where bony birds quiver
They glide through the air.
Silently humming
A horrible tune,
They sweep through the stillness
To sit on the moon.

Karla Kuskin

THE PEOPLE UPSTAIRS

The people upstairs all practise ballet.
Their living room is a bowling alley.
Their bedroom is full of conducted tours.
Their radio is louder than yours.
They celebrate weekends all the week.
When they take a shower, your ceilings leak.
They try to get their parties to mix
By supplying their guests with Pogo sticks,
And when their orgy at last abates,
They go to the bathroom on roller skates.
I might love the people upstairs wondrous
If instead of above us, they just lived under us.

Ogden Nash

LADYBIRD

Tiniest of turtles!
Your shining back
Is a shell of orange
With spots of black.

How trustingly you walk
Across this land
Of hairgrass and hollows
That is my hand.

Your small wire legs,
So frail, so thin,
Their touch is swansdown
Upon my skin.

There! break out
Your wings and fly:
No tenderer creature
Beneath the sky.

Clive Sansom

PADDINGTON ABROAD

'Delicious,' said Mr Brown. 'Very meaty and done to a turn.'

'In fact,' he continued, as he held out his plate for a second helping, 'I don't know when I've tasted anything quite so nice before.'

'Most unusual,' he went on, as he wiped his plate clean with a piece of bread and looked hopefully at the saucepan once again. 'What was it called, Paddington?'

'They're called *esca . . . esca . . .* something, Mr Brown,' said Paddington, consulting his cookery book. '*Escargots.*'

'*Escargots?*' repeated Mr Brown, dabbing at his moustache. 'Very nice too. We must get some of those when we're back in England, Mary . . .' His voice trailed away as he looked at his wife. Mrs Brown's face seemed to have gone a rather odd shade of green.

'Is anything the matter?' he asked, looking most concerned. 'You look quite ill.'

'Henry!' exclaimed Mrs Brown. 'Don't you know what *escargots* are?'

'Er . . . no,' said Mr Brown. 'Sounds familiar but I can't say that I do. Why?'

'They're snails.'

Michael Bond

THE BFG

'Do we really have to eat it?' Sophie said.

'You do unless you is wanting to become so thin you will be disappearing into a thick ear.'

'Into *thin air*,' Sophie said. 'A thick ear is something quite different.'

Once again that sad winsome look came into the BFG's eyes. 'Words,' he said, 'is oh such a twitch-tickling problem to me all my life. So you must simply try to be patient and stop squibbling. As I am telling you before, I know exactly what words I am wanting to say, but somehow or other they is always getting squiff-squiddled around.'

'That happens to everyone,' Sophie said.

'Not like it happens to me,' the BFG said. 'I is speaking the most terrible wigglish.'

'I think you speak beautifully,' Sophie said.

'You do?' cried the BFG, suddenly brightening. 'You really do?'

'Simply beautifully,' Sophie repeated.

Roald Dahl

WORZEL GUMMIDGE

'What's your name?' she asked.

'I'm Worzel Gummidge. I chose the name this morning. My granfer's name was Bogle.'

'Gummidge isn't a very pretty name,' objected Susan.

'No,' he replied. 'It's as ugly as I am.'

Susan looked at him. His hat was awry over his turnipy face. A shabby black coat hung from his shoulders, and one arm was still akimbo. But she noticed that he had managed to bend his knees a little, and that his fingers, which two minutes before had looked like bits of stick, were more human now; they even showed lumps that might possibly be mistaken for knuckles. He was growing less like a scarecrow every minute. Soon, thought Susan, he might look more like a man than Farmer Braithewaite.

'Gummidge isn't pretty,' she said, 'but it's a very interesting name.'

'Ooh aye!' he agreed. 'But then, I've a power of things to interest me – roots tickling and shooting, rooks lifting in the wind, rabbits here, there, and scattered in a minute. Give over now, do!' This last remark was made to the cock-robin, who was pecking at his greenly-bearded chin.

'How old are you?' asked Susan.

'All manner of ages,' replied the scarecrow. 'My face is one age, and my feet are another, and my arms are the oldest of all.'

'How very, very queer,' said Susan.

Barbara Euphan Todd

THE SECRET GARDEN

Mary's heart began to thump and her hands to shake a little in her delight and excitement. The robin kept singing and twittering away and tilting his head on one side, as if he were as excited as she was. What was this under her hands which was square and made of iron and which her fingers found a hole in?

It was the lock of the door which had been closed ten years, and she put her hand in her pocket, drew out the key, and found it fitted the keyhole. She put the key in and turned it. It took two hands to do it, but it did turn.

And then she took a long breath and looked behind her up the long walk to see if anyone was coming. No one was coming. No one ever did come, it seemed, and she took another long breath, because she could not help it, and she held back the swinging curtain of ivy and pushed back the door which opened slowly – slowly.

Then she slipped through it, and shut it behind her, and stood with her back against it, looking about her and breathing quite fast with excitement, and wonder, and delight.

She was standing *inside* the secret garden.

F. Hodgson Burnett

HOW THE CAT BECAME

Cat was a real oddity. The others didn't know what to make of him at all.

He lived in a hollow tree in the wood. Every night, when the rest of the creatures were sound asleep, he retired to the depths of his tree – then such sounds, such screechings, yowlings, wailings! The bats that slept upside-down all day long in the hollows of the tree branches awoke with a start and fled with their wing-tips stuffed into their ears. It seemed to them that Cat was having the worst nightmares ever – ten at a time.

But no. Cat was tuning his violin.

If only you could have seen him! Curled in the warm smooth hollow of his tree, gazing up through the hole at the top of the trunk, smiling at the stars, winking at the moon – his violin tucked under his chin. Ah, Cat was a happy one.

Ted Hughes

THE HOUSE AT POOH CORNER

And as they went, Tigger told Roo (who wanted to know) all about the things that Tiggers could do.

'Can they fly?' asked Roo.

'Yes,' said Tigger, 'they're very good flyers, Tiggers are. Strornry good flyers.'

'Oo!' said Roo. 'Can they fly as well as Owl?'

'Yes,' said Tigger. 'Only they don't want to.'

'Why don't they want to?'

'Well, they just don't like it, somehow.'

Roo couldn't understand this, because he thought it would be lovely to be able to fly, but Tigger said it was difficult to explain to anybody who wasn't a Tigger himself.

'Well,' said Roo, 'can they jump as far as Kangas?'

'Yes,' said Tigger. 'When they want to.'

'I *love* jumping,' said Roo. 'Let's see who can jump farthest, you or me.'

'*I* can,' said Tigger. 'But we mustn't stop now, or we shall be late.'

'Late for what?'

'For whatever we want to be in time for,' said Tigger, hurrying on.

In a little while they came to the Six Pine Trees.

'I can swim,' said Roo. 'I fell into the river, and I swimmed. Can Tiggers swim?'

'Of course they can. Tiggers can do everything.'

A. A. Milne

ANNE OF GREEN GABLES

'Well, they didn't pick you for your looks, that's sure and certain,' was Mrs Rachel Lynde's emphatic comment. Mrs Rachel was one of those delightful and popular people who pride themselves on speaking their mind without fear or favour. 'She's terrible skinny and homely, Marilla. Come here, child, and let me have a look at you. Lawful heart, did anyone ever see such freckles? And hair as red as carrots! Come here, child, I say.'

Anne 'came there', but not exactly as Mrs Rachel expected. With one bound she crossed the kitchen floor and stood before Mrs Rachel, her face scarlet with anger, her lips quivering, and her whole slender form trembling from head to foot.

'I hate you,' she cried in a choked voice, stamping her foot on the floor. 'I hate you – I hate you – I hate you –' a louder stamp with each assertion of hatred. 'How dare you call me

33

skinny and ugly? How dare you say I'm freckled and red-headed? You are a rude, impolite, unfeeling woman!'

L. M. Montgomery

THE OWL WHO WAS AFRAID OF THE DARK

Plop climbed out of the nest-hole and wobbled along the branch outside. He peeped over the edge. The world seemed to be a very long way down.

'I'm not a very good lander,' he said. 'I might spill myself.'

'Your landing will improve with practice,' said his mother. 'Look! There's a little boy down there on the edge of the wood collecting sticks. Go and talk to him about it.'

'Now?' said Plop.

'Now,' said his mother. So Plop shut his eyes, took a deep breath, and fell off his branch.

His small white wings carried him down, but, as he said, he was not a good lander. He did seven very fast somersaults past the little boy.

'Ooh!' cried the little boy. 'A giant Catherine-wheel!'

'Actually,' said the Catherine-wheel, picking himself up, 'I'm a Barn Owl.'

Jill Tomlinson

THE MICROBE

The Microbe is so very small
You cannot make him out at all,
But many sanguine people hope
To see him through a microscope.
His jointed tongue that lies beneath
A hundred curious rows of teeth;
His seven tufted tails with lots
Of lovely pink and purple spots,
On each of which a pattern stands,
Composed of forty separate bands;
His eyebrows of a tender green;
All these have never yet been seen —
But Scientists, who ought to know,
Assure us that they must be so . . .
Oh! let us never, never doubt
What nobody is sure about!

Hilaire Belloc

MAGGIE AND MILLY
AND MOLLY AND MAY

maggie and milly and molly and may
went down to the beach (to play one day)

and maggie discovered a shell that sang
so sweetly she couldn't remember her troubles, and

milly befriended a stranded star
whose rays five languid fingers were;

and molly was chased by a horrible thing
which raced sideways while blowing bubbles: and

may came home with a smooth round stone
as small as a world and as large as alone.

For whatever we lose (like a you or a me)
it's always ourselves we find in the sea

e. e. cummings

FIVE EYES

In Hans' old mill his three black cats
Watch his bins for the thieving rats.
Whisker and claw, they crouch in the night,
Their five eyes smouldering green and bright:
Squeaks from the flour sacks, squeaks from where
The cold wind stirs on the empty stair,
Squeaking and scampering, everywhere.
Then down they pounce, now in, now out,
At whisking tail, and sniffing snout;
While lean old Hans he snores away
Till peep of light at break of day;
Then up he climbs to his creaking mill,
Out come his cats all grey with meal –
Jekkel, and Jessup, and one-eyed Jill.

Walter de la Mare

SNOW

No breath of wind,
No gleam of sun –
Still the white snow
Whirls softly down –
Twig and bough
And blade and thorn
All in an icy
Quiet, forlorn.
Whispering, rustling,
Through the air,
On sill and stone,

Roof – everywhere,
It heaps its powdery
Crystal flakes,
Of every tree
A mountain makes;
Till pale and faint
At shut of day
Stoops from the West
One wintry ray.
And, feathered in fire,
Where ghosts the moon,
A robin shrills
His lonely tune.

Walter de la Mare

LIKE RAIN IT SOUNDED

Like Rain it sounded till it curved
And then I knew 'twas Wind –
It walked as wet as any Wave
But swept as dry as sand –
When it had pushed itself away
To some remotest Plain
A coming as of Hosts was heard
That was indeed the Rain –
It filled the Wells, it pleased the Pools
It warbled in the Road –
It pulled the spigot from the Hills
And let the Floods abroad, –
It loosened acres, lifted seas
The sites of Centres stirred
Then like Elijah rode away
Upon a Wheel of Cloud.

Emily Dickinson

AT THE RAILWAY STATION, UPWAY

'There is not much that I can do,
    For I've no money that's quite my own!'
    Spoke up the pitying child –
A little boy with a violin
At the station before the train came in, –
'But I can play my fiddle to you,
And a nice one 'tis, and good in tone!'

    The man in the handcuffs smiled;
The constable looked, and he smiled, too,
    As the fiddle began to twang;
And the man in the handcuffs suddenly sang
            With grimful glee:
            'This life so free
            Is the thing for me!'
And the constable smiled, and said no word,
As if unconscious of what he heard;
And so they went on till the train came in –
The convict, and boy with the violin.

Thomas Hardy

THE FAMOUS HUMAN CANNONBALL

The famous human cannonball
stands at the cannon's side.
He's very round and very small
and very dignified.

He bows to the east, he bows to the west,
he bows to the north and south,
then proudly puffing up his chest
he steps to the cannon's mouth.

The famous human cannonball
is ready to begin.
His helpers hoist him at his call
and gently stuff him in.

The air is filled with 'ahhs' and 'ohhs'
preparing for the thrill,
but when his helpers light the fuse
the audience is still.

Then in the hushed and darkened hall
the mighty cannon roars,
the famous human cannonball
shoots out and swiftly soars.

Higher and higher the cannonball flies
in a brilliant aerial burst
and catapulting through the skies
he lands in the net – feet first.

Jack Prelutsky

THE MARROG

My desk's at the back of the class
And nobody nobody knows
I'm a Marrog from Mars
With a body of brass
And seventeen fingers and toes.
Wouldn't they shriek if they knew
I've three eyes at the back of my head
And my hair is bright purple
My nose is deep blue
And my teeth are half yellow half red?
My five arms are silver with knives on them sharper than
    spears.
I could go back right now if I liked –
And return in a million light years.
I could gobble them all for
I'm seven foot tall
And I'm breathing green flames from my ears.
Wouldn't they yell if they knew
If they guessed that a Marrog was here?
Ha-ha they haven't a clue –
Or wouldn't they tremble with fear!

Look, look, a Marrog
They'd all scrum and shout.
The blackboard would fall and the ceiling would crack
And the teacher would faint I suppose.
But I grin to myself sitting right at the back
And nobody nobody knows.

R. C. Scriven

ST MARK

And he commanded them to make all sit down by com-
panies upon the green grass. And they sat down in ranks by
hundreds, and by fifties. And when he had taken the five
loaves and the two fishes, he looked up to heaven and
blessed, and brake the loaves, and gave them to his disciples
to set before them; and the two fishes divided he among
them all. And they did all eat, and were filled. And they took
up twelve baskets full of the fragments, and of the fishes.
And they that did eat of the loaves were about five thousand
men. And straightway he constrained his disciples to get into
the ship, and to go to the other side before unto Bethsaida,
while he sent away the people. And when he had sent them
away, he departed into a mountain to pray. And when even
was come, the ship was in the midst of the sea, and he alone
on the land.

JUST WILLIAM

He set off to school with an air of injured innocence – and
the balloon. Observing an elderly and irascible-looking
gentleman in front of him, he went a few steps down a back
street, blew up his balloon, and held it tightly under his coat.
Then, when abreast of the old gentleman, he let it off. The
old gentleman gave a leap into the air and glared fiercely
around. He glanced at the small virtuous-looking schoolboy
with obviously no instrument of torture at his lips, and then

concentrated his glare of fury and suspicion on the upper windows. William hastened on to the next pedestrian. He had quite a happy walk to school.

School was at first equally successful. William opened his desk, hastily inflated his balloon, closed his desk, then gazed round with his practised expression of horrified astonishment at what followed. He drove the French master to distraction.

'Step out 'oo makes the noise,' he screamed.

No one stepped out, and the noise continued at intervals.

The mathematics master finally discovered and confiscated the balloon.

Richmal Crompton

THE BFG

Directly in front of them, lying against the side of the mountain, Sophie could see a massive round stone. It was as big as a house. The Giant reached out and rolled the stone to one side as easily as if it had been a football, and now, where the stone had been, there appeared a vast black hole. The hole was so large the Giant didn't even have to duck his head as he went in. He strode into the black hole still carrying Sophie in one hand, the trumpet and the suitcase in the other.

As soon as he was inside, he stopped and turned and rolled the great stone back into place so that the entrance to his secret cave was completely hidden from outside.

Now that the entrance had been sealed up, there was not a glint of light inside the cave. All was black.

Sophie felt herself being lowered to the ground. Then the Giant let go the blanket completely. His footsteps moved away. Sophie sat there in the dark, shivering with fear.

He is getting ready to eat me, she told herself. He will probably eat me raw, just as I am.

Or perhaps he will boil me first.

Or he will have me fried. He will drop me like a rasher of

bacon into some gigantic frying-pan sizzling with fat. A blaze of light suddenly lit up the whole place. Sophie blinked and stared.

Roald Dahl

EMIL AND THE DETECTIVES

A number 177 tram, made up of two cars linked together, drew up opposite the station. The man hesitated, and then got into the front part and sat down in a window seat.

Emil snatched up his case, put down his head, and plunged out into the street. He reached the tram just as it was going to start, but he had time to push his suitcase on to the platform of the rear part, and scrambled up after it – breathless but triumphant!

What next, he wondered? If the thief jumped off while the tram was going, he might as well give up the money as lost for ever. It would be too dangerous to follow him, hampered as he was with the suitcase.

Motor cars rushed past with horns honking and screeching brakes. They signalled right-hand turns and left-hand turns, and swung off down side streets while other cars came swooping up behind them. The noise was inde-scribable, and on the pavements crowds of people kept hurrying by. Out of every turning vans and lorries, trams and double-decker buses swarmed into the main thorough-fare. There were newspaper stands at every corner, with men shouting the latest headlines. Wherever Emil looked there were gay shop windows filled with flowers and fruit, books, clothes, fine silk underwear, gold watches and clocks. And all the buildings stretched up and up into the sky.

So this was Berlin!

Erich Kästner

And that would have been the very end of the story if it hadn't been that they felt they really must explain to the Professor why four of the coats out of his wardrobe were missing. And the Professor, who was a very remarkable man, didn't tell them not to be silly or not to tell lies, but believed the whole story. 'No,' he said, 'I don't think it will be any good trying to go back through the wardrobe door to get the coats. You won't get into Narnia again by *that* route. Nor would the coats be much use by now if you did! Eh? What's that? Yes, of course you'll get back to Narnia again some day. Once a King in Narnia, always a King in Narnia. But don't go trying to use the same route twice. Indeed, don't *try* to get there at all. It'll happen when you're not looking for it. And don't talk too much about it even among yourselves. And don't mention it to anyone else unless you find that they've had adventures of the same sort themselves. What's that? How will you know? Oh, you'll *know* all right. Odd things they say – even their looks – will let the secret out. Keep your eyes open. Bless me, what *do* they teach them at these schools?'

And that is the very end of the adventure of the wardrobe. But if the Professor was right it was only the beginning of the adventures of Narnia.

C. S. Lewis

PIPPI LONGSTOCKING

When the act was finished, the ringmaster bowed beauti-fully, and the horses trotted out. A second later the curtain opened again for a coal-black horse, and on his back stood a beautiful lady dressed in green silk tights. Her name was Miss Carmencita, it said in the programme.

The horse trotted round in the sawdust, and Miss Carmencita stood there calmly and smiled. But then some-thing happened. Just as the horse passed Pippi's place, something came whistling through the air. It was none other than Pippi herself. There she suddenly stood on the horse's back behind Miss Carmencita. At first, Miss Carmencita was so astonished that she nearly fell off the horse. Then she became angry. She began to hit behind herself with her hands in order to get Pippi to jump off. But she couldn't manage it.

'Calm down a little,' said Pippi. 'You're not the only one who's going to have fun. There are others who've paid *their* money too, believe it or not!'

Then Miss Carmencita wanted to jump off herself, but she couldn't do that either, for Pippi had a steady hold round her waist. The people in the circus couldn't help laughing. It looked so silly, they thought, to see the beautiful Miss Carmencita held fast by a little red-headed scamp who stood on the horse's back in her big shoes looking as if she'd never done anything *but* perform in a circus.

Astrid Lindgren

THE RAILWAY CHILDREN

At first they enjoyed looking out of the window, but when it grew dusk they grew sleepier and sleepier, and no one knew how long they had been in the train when they were roused by Mother's shaking them gently and saying:

'Wake up, dears. We're there.'

They woke up, cold and melancholy, and stood shivering on the draughty platform while the baggage was taken out of the train. Then the engine, puffing and blowing, set to work again, and dragged the train away. The children watched the tail-lights of the guard's van disappear into the darkness.

This was the first train the children saw on that railway which was in time to become so very dear to them. They did not guess then how they would grow to love the railway, and how soon it would become the centre of their new life nor what wonders and changes it would bring to them. They only shivered and sneezed and hoped the walk to the new house would not be long. Peter's nose was colder than he ever remembered it to have been before. Roberta's hat was crooked, and the elastic seemed tighter than usual. Phyllis's shoe-laces had come undone.

'Come,' said Mother, 'we've got to walk. There aren't any cabs here.'

E. Nesbit

TREASURE ISLAND

The red glare of the torch, lighting up the interior of the blockhouse, showed me the worst of my apprehensions realized. The pirates were in possession of the house and stores; there was the cask of cognac, there were the pork and bread, as before; and, what tenfold increased my horror, not a sign of any prisoner. I could only judge that all had perished, and my heart smote me sorely that I had not been there to perish with them.

There were six of the buccaneers, all told; not another man was left alive. Five of them were on their feet, flushed and swollen, suddenly called out of the first sleep of drunkenness. The sixth had only risen upon his elbow: he was deadly pale, and the blood-stained bandage round his head told that he had recently been wounded, and still more recently dressed. I remembered the man who had been shot and had run back among the woods in the great attack, and doubted not that this was he.

The parrot sat, preening her plumage, on Long John's shoulder. He himself, I thought, looked somewhat paler and more stern than I was used to. He still wore the fine broadcloth suit in which he had fulfilled his mission, but it was bitterly the worse for wear, daubed with clay and torn with the sharp briers of the wood.

Robert Louis Stevenson

THE LLAMA

The Llama is a woolly sort of fleecy hairy goat,
With an indolent expression and an undulating throat
   Like an unsuccessful literary man.
And I know the place he lives in (or at least – I think I do)
It is Ecuador, Brazil or Chili – possibly Peru;
   You must find it in the Atlas if you can.
The Llama of the Pampasses you never should confound
(In spite of a deceptive similarity of sound)
   With the Lhama who is Lord of Turkestan.
For the former is a beautiful and valuable beast
But the latter is not lovable nor useful in the least;
And the Ruminant is preferable surely to the Priest
Who battens on the woeful superstititions of the East
   The Mongol of the Monastery of Shan.

Hilaire Belloc

ON A NIGHT OF SNOW

Cat, if you go out-doors you must walk in the snow.
You will come back with little white shoes on your feet,
Little white slippers of snow that have heels of sleet.
Stay by the fire, my Cat. Lie still, do not go.
See how the flames are leaping and hissing low,
I will bring you a saucer of milk like a marguerite,
So white and so smooth, so spherical and so sweet –
Stay with me, Cat. Out-doors the wild winds blow.

Out-doors the wild winds blow, Mistress, and dark is
   the night.
Strange voices cry in the trees, intoning strange lore,
And more than cats move, lit by our eyes' green light,
On silent feet where the meadow grasses hang hoar –

46

Mistress, there are portents abroad of magic and might,
And things that are yet to be done. Open the door!

Elizabeth J. Coatsworth

STOPPING BY WOODS ON A SNOWY EVENING

Whose woods these are I think I know.
His house is in the village though;
He will not see me stopping here
To watch his woods fill up with snow.

My little horse must think it queer
To stop without a farmhouse near
Between the woods and frozen lake
The darkest evening of the year.

He gives his harness bells a shake
To ask if there is some mistake.
The only other sound's the sweep
Of easy wind and downy flake.

The woods are lovely, dark and deep.
But I have promises to keep,
And miles to go before I sleep,
And miles to go before I sleep.

Robert Frost

WEATHERS

This is the weather the cuckoo likes,
        And so do I;
When showers betumble the chestnut spikes,
        And nestlings fly:
And the little brown nightingale bills his best,
And they sit outside at 'The Travellers' Rest',
And maids come forth sprig-muslin drest,
And citizens dream of the south and west,
        And so do I.

This is the weather the shepherd shuns,
    And so do I;
When beeches drip in browns and duns,
    And thresh, and ply;
And hill-hid tides throb, throe on throe,
And meadow rivulets overflow,
And drops on gate-bars hang in a row,
And rooks in families homeward go,
    And so do I.

Thomas Hardy

PRINCE KANO

In a dark wood Prince Kano lost his way
And searched in vain through the long summer's day.
At last, when night was near, he came in sight
Of a small clearing filled with yellow light,
And there, bending beside his brazier stood
A charcoal burner wearing a black hood.
The Prince cried out for joy: 'Good friend, I'll give
What you will ask: guide me to where I live.'
The man pulled back his hood: he had no face –
Where it should be there was an empty space.

Half dead with fear the Prince staggered away,
Rushed blindly through the wood till break of day;
And then he saw a larger clearing, filled
With houses, people; but his soul was chilled.
He looked around for comfort, and his search
Led him inside a small, half-empty church
Where monks prayed. 'Father,' to one he said,
'I've seen a dreadful thing; I am afraid.'
'What did you see, my son?' 'I saw a man
Whose face was like . . .' and, as the Prince began,
The monk drew back his hood and seemed to hiss,
Pointing to where his face should be, 'Like this?'

Edward Lowbury

48

OCTOBER

I've brought you nuts and hops;
    And when the leaf drops, why, the walnut drops.
Crack your first nut and light your first fire,
    Roast your first chestnut crisp on the bar;
Make the logs sparkle, stir the blaze higher,
      Logs are as cheery as sun or as star,
      Logs we can find wherever we are.
      Spring one soft day will open the leaves,
Spring one bright day will lure back the flowers;
    Never fancy my whistling wind grieves,
Never fancy I've tears in my showers:
Dance, night and days! and dance on, my hours!

Christina Rossetti

FLIGHT OF THE ROLLER-COASTER

Once more around should do it, the man confided . . .

and sure enough, when the roller-coaster reached the
    peak
of the giant curve above me, screech of its wheels almost
    drowned out by the shriller cries of the riders,

instead of the dip and plunge with its landslide of
    screams,
it rose in the air like a movieland magic carpet, some
    wonderful bird,

and without fuss or fanfare swooped slowly across the
    amusement-park,
over Spook's Castle, ice-cream booths, shooting-gallery.
And losing no height

made the last yards above the beach, where the
    cucumber-cool
brakeman in the last seat saluted
a lady about to change from her bathing-suit.

Then, as many witnesses reported, headed leisurely out
    over the water,
disappearing all too soon behind a low-flying flight of
    clouds.

Raymond Souster

THE SONG OF THE WHALE

Heaving mountain in the sea,
Whale, I heard you
Grieving.

Great whale, crying for your life,
Crying for your kind, I knew
How we would use
Your dying:

Lipstick for our painted faces,
Polish for our shoes.

Tumbling mountain in the sea,
Whale, I heard you
Calling.

Bird-high notes, keening, soaring:
At their edge a tiny drum
Like a heartbeat.

We would make you
Dumb.

In the forest of the sea,
Whale, I heard you
Singing,

Singing to your kind.
We'll never let you be.
Instead of life we choose

Lipstick for our painted faces
Polish for our shoes.

Kit Wright

EXODUS

And when she could not longer hide him, she took for him an ark of bulrushes, and daubed it with slime and with pitch, and put the child therein; and she laid it in the flags by the river's brink. And his sister stood afar off, to wit what would be done to him. And the daughter of Pharaoh came down to wash herself at the river; and her maidens walked along by the river's side; and when she saw the ark among the flags, she sent her maid to fetch it. And when she had opened it, she saw the child: and, behold, the babe wept. And she had compassion on him, and said, This is one of the Hebrews' children. Then said his sister to Pharaoh's daughter, Shall I go and call to thee a nurse of the Hebrew women, that she may nurse the child for thee? And Pharaoh's daughter said to her, Go. And the maid went and called the child's mother. And Pharaoh's daughter said unto her, Take this child away, and nurse it for me, and I will give thee thy wages. And the woman took the child, and nursed it. And the child grew, and she brought him unto Pharaoh's daughter, and he became her son. And she called his name Moses: and she said, Because I drew him out of the water.

I AM THE CHEESE

The dog is ferocious and I am terrified.

He is waiting for me at the end of a long flat stretch at the bottom of the hill. I had seen him waiting for a long distance when he was only a small, silent lump at the side of the road. Then, as I drew nearer, he revealed himself as a German shepherd, sleek and black, a silent sentinel guarding the driveway of a big white house. The house is set back from the road. I sense that the house is deserted, that I am alone out here with the dog. I pump furiously, wanting to sail by the dog as fast as possible, so fast that I will dazzle him with my speed and leave him stunned by my passing.

The dog lifts his head at my approach, alert, ears sharp, as if he is accepting a challenge. My eyes swing quickly, left to right and back again, but there are no rescuers in sight.

Robert Cormier

CRANFORD

The whole town knew and kindly regarded Miss Betsy Barker's Alderney; therefore great was the sympathy and regret when, in an unguarded moment, the poor cow tumbled into a lime-pit. She moaned so loudly that she was soon heard and rescued; but meanwhile the poor beast had lost most of her hair, and came out looking naked, cold, and miserable, in a bare skin. Everybody pitied the animal, though a few could not restrain their smiles at her droll appearance. Miss Betsy Barker absolutely cried with sorrow and dismay; and it was said she thought of trying a bath of oil. This remedy, perhaps, was recommended by some one of the number whose advice she asked; but the proposal, if ever it was made, was knocked on the head by Captain Brown's decided, 'Get her a flannel coat and flannel drawers, ma'am, if you wish to keep her alive. But my advice is, kill the poor creature at once.'

Miss Betsy Barker dried her eyes, and thanked the Captain heartily; she set to work, and by and by all the town turned out to see the Alderney meekly going to her pasture, clad in dark grey flannel. I have watched her myself, many a time. Do you ever see cows dressed in grey flannel in London?

Mrs Gaskell

THE IRON MAN

Hogarth carefully quietly hardly breathing climbed slowly down the tree. He must get home and tell his father. But at the bottom of the tree he stopped. He could no longer see the Iron Man against the twilight sky. Had he gone back over the cliff into the sea? Or was he coming down the hill, in the darkness under that high skyline, towards Hogarth and the farms?

Then Hogarth understood what was happening. He could hear a strange tearing and creaking sound. The Iron Man was pulling up the barbed-wire fence that led down the hill. And soon Hogarth could see him, as he came nearer, tearing the wire from the fence posts, rolling it up like spaghetti and eating it. The Iron Man was eating the barbed fencing wire.

But if he went along the fence, eating as he moved, he wouldn't come anywhere near the trap, which was out in the middle of the field. He could spend the whole night wandering about the countryside along the fences, rolling up the wire and eating it, and never would any fence bring him near the trap.

But Hogarth had an idea. In his pocket, among other things, he had a long nail and a knife. He took these out. Did he dare? His idea frightened him. In the silent dusk, he tapped the nail and the knife blade together.

Clink, Clink, Clink!

Ted Hughes

A WIZARD OF EARTHSEA

He turned the boat around, working her carefully round with spell and with makeshift oar lest she knock up against the underwater rocks or be entangled in the outreaching roots and branches, till she faced outward again; and he was about to raise up a wind to take him back as he had come, when suddenly the words of the spell froze on his lips, and his heart went cold within him. He looked back over his shoulder. The shadow stood behind him in the boat.

Had he lost one instant, he had been lost; but he was ready, and lunged to seize and hold the thing which wavered and trembled there within arm's reach. No wizardry would serve him now, but only his own flesh, his life itself, against the unliving. He spoke no word, but attacked, and the boat plunged and pitched from his sudden turn and lunge. And a pain ran up his arms into his breast, taking away his breath, and an icy cold filled him, and he was blinded; yet in his hands that seized the shadow there was nothing – darkness, air.

Ursula LeGuin

SWALLOWDALE

Two whistles sounded shrilly, and the whole party burst out through the bushes and charged with a yell into their ancient camping-ground. Five tents had been set up there, four small ones, where the Swallows' tents had been before the ship-wreck, and a large one, where the Amazons' tent had been the year before. A sixth tent was behind the others, among the trees.

'They've got tents just like ours,' said Roger, as he swung desperately from foot to crutch and from crutch to foot, determined not to be last.

Nancy and Peggy charged at the big tent. The others rushed past the fireplace, across the open ground.

'But they *are* ours,' said Susan.

'Pretty Polly!' said a harsh voice.

The camp had no defenders. The fire in Susan's old fireplace had burned very low, and at the farther side of the camp with his back propped against a tree, was Captain Flint, just opening his eyes, while the ship's parrot, perched beside him on one of the roots of the tree, was trying to pull his pipe to pieces.

'Hullo,' said Captain Flint, 'what time is it? I sat down for a minute to play with old Polly. Hot work, you know, shifting all these things down to the launch, and that tree takes some climbing, too. Why, what on earth's the matter with you all?'

The Swallows and Amazons looked at each other.

'Oh, nothing,' said Captain Nancy. 'We mistook you for somebody else.'

Arthur Ransome

Above everything I could hear the querulous tones of Gran, going over and over again: 'What's he on about? What's he on about? What's he on about? What's he on about?'

I took a deep breath and made it obvious that I was taking a deep breath, and said: 'Look, there is a comedian. The comedian's name is Danny Boon. B–double-O–N. He does not write his own scripts. He gets other people to do it for him. He likes my material. He thinks he can give me regular work.'

My mother said: 'How do you mean, he likes your material?'

I brought out the heavy sigh and the clenched teeth. 'Look. This pepper-pot is Danny Boon. This salt-cellar is my material. Danny Boon is looking for material –' I turned the blue plastic pepper-pot on them like a ray-gun. 'He sees my flaming material. So he flaming well asks for it.'

' 'Ere, rear, rear, watch your bloody language! With your flaming this and flaming that! At meal-times! You're not in bloody London yet, you know!'

Keith Waterhouse

THE REMARKABLE ROCKET

The Rocket was very damp, so he took a long time to burn. At last, however, the fire caught him.

'Now I am going off!' he cried, and he made himself very stiff and straight. 'I know I shall go much higher than the stars, much higher than the moon, much higher than the sun. In fact, I shall go so high that –'

Fizz! Fizz! Fizz! and he went straight up into the air.

'Delightful!' he cried, 'I shall go on like this for ever. What a success I am!'

But nobody saw him.

Then he began to feel a curious tingling sensation all over him.

'Now I am going to explode,' he cried. 'I shall set the whole world on fire, and make such a noise that nobody will talk about anything else for a whole year.' And he certainly did explode. Bang! Bang! Bang! went his gunpowder. There was no doubt about it.

But nobody heard him, not even the two little boys, for they were sound asleep.

Then all that was left of him was the stick, and this fell down on the back of a Goose who was taking a walk by the side of the ditch.

'Good heavens!' cried the Goose. 'It is going to rain sticks;' and she rushed into the water.

'I knew I should create a great sensation,' gasped the Rocket, and he went out.

Oscar Wilde

TIMOTHY WINTERS

Timothy Winters comes to school
With eyes as wide as a football-pool,
Ears like bombs and teeth like splinters:
A blitz of a boy is Timothy Winters.

His belly is white, his neck is dark,
And his hair is an exclamation-mark.
His clothes are enough to scare a crow
And through his britches the blue winds blow.

When teacher talks he won't hear a word
And he shoots down dead the arithmetic-bird,
He licks the patterns off his plate
And he's not even heard of the Welfare State.

Timothy Winters has bloody feet
And he lives in a house on Suez Street,
He sleeps in a sack on the kitchen floor
And they say there aren't boys like him any more.

Old Man Winters likes his beer
And his missus ran off with a bombardier,
Grandma sits in the grate with a gin
And Timothy's dosed with an aspirin.

The Welfare Worker lies awake
But the law's as tricky as a ten-foot snake,
So Timothy Winters drinks his cup
And slowly goes on growing up.

At Morning Prayers the Master helves
For children less fortunate than ourselves,
And the loudest response in the room is when
Timothy Winters roars 'Amen!'

So come one angel, come on ten:
Timothy Winters says 'Amen,
Amen, amen, amen, amen.'
Timothy Winters, Lord.
                    Amen.

                              Charles Causley

GUS: THE THEATRE CAT

Gus is the Cat at the Theatre Door.
His name, as I ought to have told you before,
Is really Asparagus. That's such a fuss
To pronounce, that we usually call him just Gus.
His coat's very shabby, he's thin as a rake,
And he suffers from palsy that makes his paw shake.
Yet he was, in his youth, quite the smartest of Cats –
But no longer a terror to mice and to rats.
For he isn't the Cat that he was in his prime;
Though his name was quite famous, he says, in its time.
And whenever he joins his friends at their club
(Which takes place at the back of the neighbouring pub)
He loves to regale them, if someone else pays,
With anecdotes drawn from his palmiest days.
For he once was a Star of the highest degree –
He has acted with Irving, he's acted with Tree.
And he likes to relate his success on the Halls,
Where the Gallery once gave him seven cat-calls
But his grandest creation, as he loves to tell,
Was Firefrorefiddle, the Fiend of the Fell.

                              T. S. Eliot

TROUT

Hangs, a fat gun-barrel,
deep under arched bridges
or slips like butter down
the throat of the river.

From the depths smooth-skinned as plums
his muzzle gets bull's eye;
picks off grass-seed and moths
that vanish, torpedoed.

Where water unravels
over gravel-bed he
is fired from the shallows
white belly reporting

flat; darts like a tracer-
bullet back between stones
and is never burnt out.
A volley of cold blood

ramrodding the current.

Seamus Heaney

A BOY'S HEAD

In it there is a space-ship
and a project
for doing away with piano lessons.

And there is
Noah's ark,
which shall be first.

And there is
an entirely new bird,
an entirely new hare,
an entirely new bumble-bee.

There is a river
that flows upwards.

There is a multiplication table.

There is anti-matter.

And is just cannot be trimmed.

I believe
that only what cannot be trimmed
is a head.
There is much promise
in the circumstance
that so many people have heads.

Miroslav Holub

OWL

A shadow is floating through the moonlight.
Its wings don't make a sound.
Its claws are long, its beak is bright.
Its eyes try all the corners of the night.

It calls and calls: all the air swells and heaves
And washes up and down like water.
The ear that listens to the owl believes
In death. The bat beneath the eaves,

The mouse beside the stone are still as death —
The owl's air washes them like water.
The owl goes back and forth inside the night,
And the night holds its breath.

Randall Jarrell

GOOD TASTE

Travelling, a man met a tiger, so . . .
He ran. The tiger ran after him
Thinking: How fast I run . . . But

The road thought: How long I am . . . Then,
They came to a cliff, yes, the man
Grabbed at an ash root and swung down

Over its edge. Above his knuckles, the tiger.
At the foot of the cliff, its mate. Two mice,
One black, one white, began to gnaw the root.

And by the traveller's head grew one
Juicy strawberry, so . . . hugging the root
The man reached out and plucked the fruit.
        How sweet it tasted!

Christopher Logue

YOU'D BETTER BELIEVE HIM
A Fable

Discovered an old rocking-horse in Woolworth's,
He tried to feed it but without much luck
So he stroked it, had a long conversation about
The trees it came from, the attics it had visited.
Tried to take it out then
But the store detective he
Called the police who in court next morning said
'He acted strangely when arrested,
His statement read simply "I believe in rocking-
horses."
We have reason to believe him mad.'
'Quite so,' said the prosecution,
'Bring in the rocking-horse as evidence.'
'I'm afraid it's escaped, sir,' said the store manager,
'Left a hoof print as evidence
On the skull of the store detective.'
'Quite so,' said the prosecution, fearful
of the neighing
Out in the corridor.

Brian Patten

THE GREY HORSE

A dappled horse stood at the edge of the meadow,
He was peaceful and quiet and grey as a shadow.
Something he seemed to be saying to me,
As he stood in the shade of the chestnut tree.

'It's a wonderful morning,' he seemed to say,
'So jump on my back, and let's be away!
It's over the hedge and we'll leap and fly,
And up the hill to the edge of the sky.

'For over the hill there are fields without end;
On the galloping downs we can run like the wind.
Down pathways we'll canter, by streams we'll stray,
Oh, jump on my back and let's be away!'

As I went by the meadow one fine summer morn,
The grey horse had gone like a ghost with the dawn;
He had gone like a ghost and not waited for me,
And it's over the hilltop he'd surely be.

James Reeves

RUTH

Turn again, my daughters, go your way; for I am too old to
have an husband. If I should say, I have hope, if I should
have an husband also to night, and should also bear sons;
Would ye tarry for them till they were grown? would ye stay
for them from having husbands? nay, my daughters; for it
grieveth me much for your sakes that the hand of the Lord is
gone out against me. And they lifted up their voice, and wept
again: and Orpah kissed her mother in law; but Ruth clave
unto her. And she said, Behold, thy sister in law is gone back
unto her people, and unto her gods: return thou after thy
sister in law. And Ruth said, Intreat me not to leave thee, or
to return from following after thee: for whither thou goest, I
will go; and where thou lodgest, I will lodge: thy people shall
be my people, and thy God my God: Where thou diest, will I

die, and there will I be buried: the Lord do so to me, and more also, if ought but death part thee and me. When she saw that she was stedfastly minded to go with her, then she left speaking unto her.

THE HAND

'One morning towards the end of November, my servant woke me with the news that Sir John Rowell had been murdered during the night.

'Half an hour later I entered the Englishman's house with the superintendent of police and the captain of the local gendarmes. Sir John's valet was weeping outside the door, utterly distraught. At first I suspected him, but he was innocent. The murderer was never found.

'Going into the drawing-room, the first thing I saw was the corpse lying on its back in the middle of the floor.

'Sir John's waistcoat was torn and one sleeve of his coat had been practically torn off. There was every indication of a terrible struggle.

'The Englishman had been strangled. His black, swollen face was a horrible sight, and it bore an expression of appalling terror. His teeth were clenched on some object and in his neck which was covered with blood there were five holes which looked as if they had been made with iron spikes.

'We were joined by the doctor. He made a lengthy examination of the fingermarks in the flesh of the dead man's neck and then uttered these strange words: "It looks as if he had been strangled by a skeleton."

'A shiver ran down my spine, and I glanced at the wall where I had been accustomed to seeing the horrible flayed hand. The hand was no longer there. The chain had been broken and was hanging loose.'

Guy de Maupassant

There is no going back in life. There is no return. No second chance. I cannot call back the spoken word or the accomplished deed, sitting here, alive and in my own home, any more than poor Tom Jenkyn could, swinging in his chains.

It was my godfather Nick Kendall who, in his bluff straightforward fashion, said to me on the eve of my twenty-fifth birthday – a few months ago only, yet God! how long in time – 'There are some women, Philip, good women very possibly, who through no fault of their own impel disaster. Whatever they touch somehow turns to tragedy. I don't know why I say this to you, but I feel I must.' And then he witnessed my signature on the document that I had put before him.

No, there is no return. The boy who stood under her window on his birthday eve, the boy who stood within the doorway of her room the evening that she came, he has gone, just as the child has gone who threw a stone at a dead man on a gibbet to give himself false courage. Tom Jenkyn, battered specimen of humanity, unrecognizable and un-lamented, did you, all those years ago, stare after me in pity as I went running down the woods into the future?

Had I looked back at you, over my shoulder, I should not have seen you swinging in your chains, but my own shadow.

Daphne du Maurier

THE MILL ON THE FLOSS

Tom followed Maggie upstairs into her mother's room, and saw her go at once to a drawer, from which she took out a large pair of scissors.

'What are they for, Maggie?' said Tom, feeling his curiosity awakened.

Maggie answered by seizing her front locks and cutting them straight across the middle of her forehead.

'O, my buttons, Maggie, you'll catch it!' exclaimed Tom; 'you'd better not cut any more off.'

Snip! went the great scissors again while Tom was

speaking; and he couldn't help feeling it was rather good fun: Maggie would look so queer.

'Here, Tom, cut it behind for me,' said Maggie, excited by her own daring, and anxious to finish the deed.

'You'll catch it, you know,' said Tom, nodding his head in an admonitory manner, and hesitating a little as he took the scissors.

'Never mind – make haste!' said Maggie, giving a little stamp with her foot. Her cheeks were quite flushed.

The black locks were so thick – nothing could be more tempting to a lad who had already tasted the forbidden pleasure of cutting the pony's mane. I speak to those who know the satisfaction of making a pair of shears meet through a duly resisting mass of hair. One delicious grinding snip, and then another and another, and the hinder-locks fell heavily on the floor, and Maggie stood cropped in a jagged, uneven manner, but with a sense of clearness and freedom, as if she had emerged from a wood into the open plain.

George Eliot

THOMASINA

I suppose you think that checking a mousehole is easy and no work at all. Well, all I can say is *you* try it some time. Get down on your hands and knees and remain in that position, concentrating and staring at one little hole in the wainscoting for hours at a time, while simultaneously pretending that you are not. Checking a mousehole isn't just giving it a sniff and going away as a dog would do. On the contrary. If you are as conscientious and dutiful as I am, it is a full-time job, particularly if there are two or three or you suspect one of them of having two entrances.

It isn't catching mice, mind you, that is the most necessary. Anyone can catch a mouse; it is no trick at all; it is putting them off and keeping them down that is important. You will hear sayings like – 'The only good mouse is a dead mouse,' but that is only half of it. The only good mouse is the mouse that isn't there at all. What you must do if you are at all principled about your work, is to conduct a war of nerves on the creatures. This calls for both time, energy, and a good deal of cleverness which I wouldn't begrudge if I wasn't expected to do so many other things besides.

Just to give you an idea of what mousehole watching entails, after you have located and charted them and decided which ones are active and which extinct, you select one and go there, but, of course, *never* twice at the same time exactly. A mouse is no fool and soon learns to time you if you are regular. I find that hunch and instinct, or just plain feline know-how are the best things to guide you. You just *know* at a certain moment; it comes over you as in a dream that *that* is the time to go there.

Paul Gallico

LET SLEEPING VETS LIE

A prickling apprehension began to creep over me, a feeling that my living person had no place here among these brooding relics of dead centuries. I turned quickly and began to hurry through the wood, bumping into the trees, tripping over roots and bushes, and when I reached my car I was trembling and more out of breath than I should have been. It was good to slam the door, turn the ignition and hear the familiar roar of the engine.

I was home within ten minutes and trotted up the stairs, looking forward to catching up on my lost sleep. Opening my bedroom door I flicked on the switch and felt a momentary surprise when the room remained in darkness. Then I stood frozen in the doorway.

By the window, where the moonlight flooded in, making a pool of silver in the gloom, a monk was standing. A monk in a brown habit, motionless, arms folded, head bowed. His face was turned from the light towards me but I could see nothing under the drooping cowl but a horrid abyss of darkness.

I thought I would choke. My mouth opened but no sound came. And in my racing mind one thought pounded above the others — there were such things as ghosts after all.

James Herriot

THE ENCHANTED PLACES

To the left of the path as it enters the wood is a lake. If you called our river a stream then I suppose you would want to call this lake a bog. But for me it was a lake: in winter when it froze over it was possible to do some quite good sliding between the tussocks of rush. The path continues between lake and river until it is crossed by a larger track that has entered the wood over a bridge. This bridge still stands and still looks much as it did when Shepard came there to draw it: it is Poohsticks Bridge.

It is difficult to be sure which came first. Did I do something and did my father then write a story around it? Or was it the other way about, and did the story come first? Certainly my father was on the look-out for ideas; but so too was I. He wanted ideas for his stories, I wanted them for my games, and each looked towards the other for inspiration. But in the end it was all the same: the stories became a part of our lives; we lived them, thought them, spoke them. And so, possibly before, but certainly after that particular story, we used to stand on Poohsticks Bridge throwing sticks into the water and watching them float away out of sight until they re-emerged on the other side.

Christopher Milne

THE SCARLET PIMPERNEL

This incident had spoiled the afternoon. The people were terrified of these two horrible curses, the two maladies which nothing could cure, and which were the precursors of an awful and lonely death. They hung about the barricades, silent and sullen for a while, eyeing one another suspic-iously, avoiding each other as if by instinct, lest the plague lurked already in their midst. Presently, as in the case of Grospierre, a captain of the guard appeared suddenly. But he was known to Bibot, and there was no fear of his turning out to be a sly Englishman in disguise.

'A cart . . .' he shouted breathlessly, even before he had reached the gates.

'What cart?' asked Bibot, roughly.

'Driven by an old hag . . . A cart . . . A covered cart . . .'

'There were a dozen . . .'

'An old hag who said her son had the plague?'

'Yes . . .'

'You have not let them go?'

'*Morbleu!*' said Bibot, whose purple cheeks had suddenly become white with fear.

'The cart contained the *ci-devant* Comtesse de Tournay and her two children, all of them traitors and condemned to death.'

'And their driver?' muttered Bibot, as a superstitious shudder ran down his spine.

'*Sacré tonnerre*,' said the captain, 'but it is feared that it was that accursed Englishman himself – the Scarlet Pimpernel.'

Baroness Orczy

EXECUTIVE

I am a young executive. No cuffs than mine are cleaner;
I have a Slimline brief-case and I use the firm's Cortina.
In every roadside hostelry from here to Burgess Hill
The maitres d'hôtel all know me well and let me sign the
    bill.

You ask me what it is I do. Well actually, you know,
I'm partly a liaison man and partly P.R.O.
Essentially I integrate the current export drive
And basically I'm viable from ten o'clock till five.

For vital off-the-record work – that's talking
    transport-wise –
I've a scarlet Aston-Martin – and does she go? She flies!
Pedestrians and dogs and cats – we mark them down for
    slaughter.
I also own a speed-boat which has never touched the
    water.

She's built of fibre-glass, of course. I call her 'Mandy
    Jane'
After a bird I used to know – No soda, please, just plain –
And how did I acquire her? Well to tell you about that
And to put you in the picture I must wear my other hat.

I do some mild developing. The sort of place I need
Is a quiet country market town that's rather run to seed.
A luncheon and a drink or two, a little savoir faire –
I fix the Planning Officer, the Town Clerk and the
    Mayor.

And if some preservationist attempts to interfere
A 'dangerous structure' noticed from the Borough
   Engineer
Will settle any buildings that are standing in our way –
The modern style, sir, with respect, has really come to
   stay.

John Betjeman

WHO

Who is that child I see wandering, wandering
Down by the side of the quivering stream?
Why does he seem not to hear, though I call to him?
Where does he come from, and what is his name?

Why do I see him at sunrise and sunset
Taking, in old-fashioned clothes, the same track?
Why, when he walks, does he cast not a shadow
Though the sun rises and falls at his back?

Why does the dust lie so thick on the hedgerow
By the great field where a horse pulls the plough?
Why do I see only meadows, where houses
Stand in a line by the riverside now?

Why does he move like a wraith by the water,
Soft as the thistledown on the breeze blown?
When I draw near him so that I may hear him,
Why does he say that his name is my own?

Charles Causley

THE LESSON

Chaos ruled O K in the classroom
as bravely the teacher walked in
the havocwreakers ignored him
his voice was lost in the din

'The theme for today is violence
and homework will be set
I'm going to teach you a lesson
one that you'll never forget'

He picked on a boy who was shouting
and throttled him then and there
then garrotted the girl behind him
(the one with the grotty hair)

Then sword in hand he hacked his way
between the chattering rows
'First come, first severed,' he declared
'fingers, feet, or toes'

He threw the sword at a latecomer
it struck with deadly aim
then pulling out a shotgun
he continued with his game

The first blast cleared the backrow
(where those who skive hang out)
they collapsed like rubber dinghies
when the plug's pulled out

'Please may I leave the room sir?'
a trembling vandal enquired
'Of course you may' said teacher
put the gun to his temple and fired

The Head popped a head round the doorway
to see why a din was being made
nodded understandingly
then tossed in a grenade

And when the ammo was well spent
with blood on every chair
Silence shuffled forward
with its hands up in the air.

The teacher surveyed the carnage
the dying and the dead
He waggled a finger severely
'Now let that be a lesson' he said.

Roger McGough

THE SHELL

And then I pressed the shell
Close to my ear,
And listened well.

And straightway, like a bell,
Came low and clear
The slow, sad murmur of far distant seas

Whipped by an icy breeze
Upon a shore
Wind-swept and desolate.

It was a sunless strand that never bore
The footprint of a man,
Nor felt the weight

Since time began
Of any human quality or stir,
Save what the dreary winds and waves incur.

And in the hush of waters was the sound
Of pebbles, rolling round;
For ever rolling, with a hollow sound:

And bubbling sea-weeds, as the waters go,
Swish to and fro
Their long, cold tentacles of slimy grey:

There was no day;
Nor ever came a night
Setting the stars alight

To wonder at the moon:
Was twilight only, and the frightened croon,
Smitten to whimpers, of the dreary wind

And waves that journeyed blind . . .
And then I loosed my ear – Oh, it was sweet
To hear a cart go jolting down the street.

James Stephens

WATER PICTURE

In the pond in the park
all things are doubled:
Long buildings hang and
wriggle gently. Chimneys
are bent legs bouncing
on clouds below. A flag
wags like a fishhook
down there in the sky.

The arched stone bridge
is an eye, with underlid
in the water. In its lens
dip crinkled heads with hats
that don't fall off. Dogs go by,
barking on their backs.
A baby, taken to feed the
ducks, dangles upside-down,
a pink balloon for a buoy.

Treetops deploy a haze of
cherry bloom for roots,
where birds coast belly-up
in the glass bowl of a hill;
from its bottom a bunch
of peanut-munching children
is suspended by their
sneakers, waveringly.

A swan, with twin necks
forming the figure three,
steers between two dimpled
towers doubled. Fondly
hissing, she kisses herself,
and all the scene is troubled:
water-windows splinter,
tree-limbs tangle, the bridge
folds like a fan.

May Swenson

IN MOONLIGHT

We sat where boughs waved on the ground
But made no sound;
'They cannot shake me off,'
Shrieked the black dwarf,
Impudent elf,
That was the shadow of myself.

I said to him, 'We must go now';
But from his bough
He laughed, securely perched,
'Then you rise first';
It seemed to me
He spoke in wicked courtesy.

We rose and 'Take my hand,' he whined,
Though like the wind
Each waving bough he leapt;
And as we stept
Down the steep track
He seemed to grow more hunched and black.

Andrew Young

AUNT JULIA

Aunt Julia spoke Gaelic
very loud and very fast.
I could not answer her –
I could not understand her.

She wore men's boots
when she wore any.
– I can see her strong foot,
stained with peat,
paddling the treadle of the spinning wheel
while her right hand drew yarn
marvellously out of the air.

Hers was the only house
where I lay at night
in the absolute darkness
of the box bed, listening to
crickets being friendly.

She was buckets
and water flouncing into them.
She was winds pouring wetly
round house-ends.
She was brown eggs, black skirts
and a keeper of threepennybits
in a teapot.

Aunt Julia spoke Gaelic
very loud and very fast.
By the time I had learned
a little, she lay
silenced in the absolute black
of a sandy grave
at Luskentyre.

But I hear her still, welcoming me
with a seagull's voice
across a hundred yards
of peatscapes and lazybeds
and getting angry, getting angry
with so many questions
unanswered.

Judith Wright

WHEN YOU ARE OLD

When you are old and grey and full of sleep,
And nodding by the fire, take down this book,
And slowly read, and dream of the soft look
Your eyes had once, and of their shadows deep.

How many loved your moments of glad grace,
And loved your beauty with love false or true,
But one man loved the pilgrim soul in you,
And loved the sorrows of your changing face;

And bending down beside the glowing bars,
Murmur, a little sadly, how Love fled
And paced upon the mountains overhead
And hid his face amid a crowd of stars.

W. B. Yeats

THE YOUNG VISITERS

Bernard placed one arm tightly round her. When will you
marry me Ethel he uttered you must be my wife it has come
to that I love you so intensly that if you say no I shall
perforce dash my body to the brink of yon muddy river he
panted wildly.

Oh dont do that implored Ethel breathing rarther hard.

Then say you love me he cried.

Oh Bernard she sighed fervently I certinly love you

madly you are to me like a Heathen god she cried looking at his manly form and handsome flashing face I will indeed marry you.

How soon gasped Bernard gazing at her intensly.

As soon as possible said Ethel gently closing her eyes.

My Darling whispered Bernard and he seiezed her in his arms we will be marrid next week.

Oh Bernard muttered Ethel this is so sudden.

No no cried Bernard and taking the bull by both horns he kissed her violently on her dainty face. My bride to be he murmered several times.

Ethel trembled with joy as she heard the mistick words.

Oh Bernard she said little did I ever dream of such as this and she suddenly fainted into his out stretched arms.

Daisy Ashford

ST MATTHEW

Then was Jesus led up of the Spirit into the wilderness to be tempted of the devil. And when he had fasted forty days and forty nights, he was afterward an hungred. And when the tempter came to him, he said, If thou be the Son of God, command that these stones be made bread. But he answered and said, It is written, Man shall not live by bread alone, but by every word that proceedeth out of the mouth of God. Then the devil taketh him up into the holy city, and setteth him on a pinnacle of the temple, And saith unto him, If thou be the Son of God, cast thyself down: for it is written, He shall give his angels charge concerning thee: and in their hands they shall bear thee up, lest at any time thou dash thy foot against a stone. Jesus said unto him, It is written again, Thou shalt not tempt the Lord thy God. Again, the devil taketh him up into an exceeding high mountain, and sheweth him all the kingdoms of the world, and the glory of them; And saith unto him, All these things will I give thee, if thou wilt fall down and worship me. Then saith Jesus unto him, Get thee hence, Satan: for it is written, Thou shalt worship the Lord thy God, and him only shalt thou serve.

Then the devil leaveth him, and, behold, angels came and ministered unto him.

MONSIGNOR QUIXOTE

'That was no tyre,' Father Leopoldo said. 'Those were gun shots.' He made for the stairs and called back over his shoulder, 'The church doors are locked. Follow me.' He ran down the passage by the guest rooms as fast as his long robe would allow him and arrived out of breath at the head of the great ceremonial staircase. The professor was close behind. 'Go and find Father Enrique. Tell him to open the church doors. If someone's been hurt we can't carry him up all these stairs.'

Father Francisco, who was in charge of the little shop near the entrance, had left his picture postcards, rosaries and liqueur bottles. He looked frightened, and scrupulously he waved his hand towards the door without breaking his vow of silence.

A small Seat car had smashed against the wall of the church. Two Guardia had left their jeep and were approaching with caution with their guns at the ready. A man with blood on his face was trying to open the door of the Seat. He called angrily to the Guardia, 'Come and help, you assassins. We are not armed.'

Father Leopoldo said, 'Are you hurt?'

'Of course I'm hurt. That's nothing. I think they've killed my friend.'

Graham Greene

THE ART OF COARSE ACTING

I would define a Coarse Actor as one who can remember the lines but not the order in which they come. It is, perhaps, not an entirely satisfactory definition, and a close friend whom I regard as easily the most desperately bad amateur actor in West Bromwich suggests that a Coarse Actor is one who can remember the pauses but not the lines.

78

However, that definition falls down because most Coarse amateurs don't have any pauses. They regard their lines rather as a machine-gunner regards a belt of ammunition: something to be shot off in the vague direction of the enemy and then replaced as rapidly as possible.

Certainly, one of the infallible signs that Coarse Drama is going on is the fact that the traditional roles of actor and audience are reversed. The actor is being himself while the audience are playing a part, heavily pretending to enjoy the show, struggling to laugh at unfunny jokes and so on. Watching a bad amateur show can be more exhausting than three hours on stage.

Perhaps it all starts at school, where in a moustache made from burnt cork the trembling infant actor is pushed reluctantly on stage to mouth his halting lines while the child playing opposite bursts into tears for some unspecified reason. It is then that he discovers, execrable though he may be, that for the first time in his life several hundred people are actually paying attention to him.

Michael Green

THE ENCHANTED PLACES

The other early addition to the family was Jessica, a donkey, and no connection whatever with Eeyore, except that she lived in a field a little like Eeyore's. It was Nanny's job, helped by Tasker and slightly helped by me, to catch her and saddle her. Sometimes this was easy, sometimes not. Our first outing was a cautious trip up the lane where, with luck, nothing too disastrous could happen. And I can still recall the horrifying moment when Jessica stopped and her legs began to sag. I was snatched from her back and Nanny and I watched, appalled, as she crumpled up on the ground, then rolled on to her side, then on to her back, then kicked up her legs in the air and let out an ear-splitting bellow, then rolled – still bellowing – from side to side, then scrambled to her feet and waited for me to remount. But Nanny said: 'I don't think you'd better, dear.' And I didn't think I'd better, either. And we all three walked home.

On subsequent trips we knew what to expect, that it was

just one of the things Jessica liked doing, and so, when her legs started sagging, I got off and waited until it was all over. Subsequent trips included our weekly visit to Hartfield, a mile away along the main road, up a steep hill, down a steep hill and in at the door of the first shop on the left hand side. Jessica needed no urging and the woman behind the counter no instructions. It was a pennyworth of bullseyes for each of us.

Christopher Milne

VANITY FAIR

'How could you do so, Rebecca?' at last she said, after a pause.

'Why, do you think Miss Pinkerton will come out and order me back to the black hole?' said Rebecca, laughing.

'No: but –'

'I hate the whole house,' continued Miss Sharp in a fury. 'I hope I may never set eyes on it again. I wish it were in the bottom of the Thames, I do; and if Miss Pinkerton were there, I wouldn't pick her out, that I wouldn't. O how I should like to see her floating in the water yonder, turban and all, with her train streaming after her, and her nose like the beak of a wherry!'

'Hush!' cried Miss Sedley.

'Why, will the black footman tell tales?' cried Miss Rebecca, laughing. 'He may go back and tell Miss Pinkerton that I hate her with all my soul, and I wish he would; and I wish I had a means of proving it, too. For two years I have only had insults and outrage from her. I have been treated worse than any servant in the kitchen. I have never had a friend or a kind word, except from you. I have been made to tend the little girls in the lower schoolroom, and to talk French to the Misses, until I grew sick of my mother-tongue. But that talking French to Miss Pinkerton was capital fun, wasn't it? She doesn't know a word of French, and was too proud to confess it. I believe it was that which made her part with me; and so thank heaven for French. *Vive la France! Vive l'Empereur! Vive Bonaparte!*'

W. M. Thackeray

'Eighteen years,' laughed Dorian Gray, with a touch of triumph in his voice. 'Eighteen years! Set me under the lamp and look at my face!'

James Vane hesitated for a moment, not understanding what was meant. Then he seized Dorian Gray and dragged him from the archway.

Dim and wavering as was the wind-blown light, yet it served to show him the hideous error, as it seemed, into which he had fallen, for the face of the man he had sought to kill had all the bloom of boyhood, all the unstained purity of youth. He seemed little older than a lad of twenty summers, hardly older, if older indeed at all, than his sister had been when they had parted so many years ago. It was obvious that this was not the man who had destroyed her life.

He loosened his hold and reeled back. 'My God! my God!' he cried, 'and I would have murdered you!'

Dorian Gray drew a long breath. 'You have been on the brink of committing a terrible crime, my man,' he said, looking at him sternly. 'Let this be a warning to you not to take vengeance into your own hands.'

'Forgive me, sir,' muttered James Vane. 'I was deceived. A chance word I heard in that damned den set me on the wrong track.'

'You had better go home, and put that pistol away, or you may get into trouble,' said Dorian, turning on his heel, and going slowly down the street.

Oscar Wilde

THE SELFISH GIANT

One winter morning he looked out of his window as he was dressing. He did not hate the Winter now, for he knew that it was merely the Spring asleep, and that the flowers were resting.

Suddenly he rubbed his eyes in wonder and looked and looked. It certainly was a marvellous sight. In the farthest corner of the garden was a tree quite covered with lovely white blossoms. Its branches were golden, and silver fruit hung down from them, and underneath it stood the little boy he had loved.

Downstairs ran the Giant in great joy, and out into the garden. He hastened across the grass, and came near to the child. And when he came quite close his face grew red with anger, and he said, 'Who hath dared to wound thee?' For on the palms of the child's hands were the prints of two nails, and the prints of two nails were on the little feet.

'Who hath dared to wound thee?' cried the Giant; 'tell me, that I may take my big sword and slay him.'

'Nay!' answered the child: 'but these are the wounds of Love.'

'Who art thou?' said the Giant, and a strange awe fell on him, and he knelt before the little child.

And the child smiled on the Giant, and said to him, 'You let me play once in your garden, to-day you shall come with me to my garden, which is Paradise.'

And when the children ran in that afternoon, they found the Giant lying dead under the tree, all covered with white blossoms.

Oscar Wilde

UNWELCOME

We were young, we were merry, we were very very wise,
  And the door stood open at our feast,
When there passed us a woman with the West in her eyes,
  And a man with his back to the East.

O, still grew the hearts that were beating so fast,
  The loudest voice was still.
The jest died away on our lips as they passed,
  And the rays of July struck chill.

The cups of red wine turned pale on the board,
  The white bread black as soot.
The hound forgot the hand of her lord,
  She fell down at his foot.

Low let me die, where the dead dog lies,
  Ere I sit me down again at a feast,
When there passes a woman with the West in her eyes,
  And a man with his back to the East.

Mary Coleridge

THE OLD SUMMERHOUSE

This blue-washed, old, thatched summerhouse –
Paint scaling, and fading from its walls –
How often from its hingeless door
I have watched – dead leaf, like the ghost of a mouse,
Rasping the worn brick floor –
The snows of the weir descending below,
And their thunderous waterfall.

Fall – fall: dark, garrulous rumour,
Until I could listen no more.
Could listen no more – for beauty with sorrow
Is a burden hard to be borne:
The evening light on the foam, and the swans, there;
That music, remote, forlorn.

Walter de la Mare

SNOW IN THE SUBURBS

Every branch big with it,
Bent every twig with it;
Every fork like a white web-foot;
Every street and pavement mute:
Some flakes have lost their way, and grope back upward,
      when
Meeting those meandering down they turn and descend
      again
The palings are glued together like a wall,
And there is no waft of wind with the fleecy fall.

A sparrow enters the tree,
Whereupon immediately
A snow-lump thrice his own light size
Descends on him and showers his head and eyes,
And over turns him,
And near inurns him,
And lights on a nether twig, when its brush
Starts off a volley of other lodging lumps with a rush.

The steps are a blanched slope,
Up which, with feeble hope,
A black cat comes, wide-eyed and thin;
And we take him in.

Thomas Hardy

BLACKBERRY-PICKING

Late August, given heavy rain and sun
For a full week, the blackberries would ripen.

At first, just one, a glossy purple clot
Among others, red, green, hard as a knot.
You ate that first one and its flesh was sweet
Like thickened wine: summer's blood was in it
Leaving stains upon the tongue and lust for
Picking. Then red ones inked up and that hunger
Sent us out with milk-cans, pea-tins, jam-pots
Where briars scratched and wet grass bleached our boots.
Round hayfields, cornfields and potato-drills
We trekked and picked until the cans were full,
Until the tinkling bottom had been covered
With green ones, and on top big dark blobs burned
Like a plate of eyes. Our hands were peppered
With thorn pricks, our palms sticky as Bluebeard's.

We hoarded the fresh berries in the byre.
But when the bath was filled we found a fur,
A rat-grey fungus, glutting on our cache.
The juice was stinking too. Once off the bush
The fruit fermented, the sweet flesh would turn sour.
I always felt like crying. It wasn't fair
That all the lovely canfuls smelt of rot.
Each year I hoped they'd keep, knew they would not.

Seamus Heaney

PIED BEAUTY

Glory be to God for dappled things –
    For skies of couple-colour as a brinded cow;
        For rose-moles all in stipple upon trout that swim;
Fresh-firecoal chestnut-falls; finches' wings;
    Landscape plotted and pieced – fold, fallow, and
    plough;
        And all trades, their gear and tackle and trim.
All things counter, original, spare, strange;
    Whatever is fickle, freckled (who knows how?)
        With swift, slow; sweet, sour; adazzle, dim;
He fathers-forth whose beauty is past change:
                    Praise him.

Gerard Manley Hopkins

85

ANNE FRANK HUIS

Even now, after twice her lifetime of grief
and anger in the very place, whoever comes
to climb these narrow stairs, discovers how
the bookcase slides aside, then walks through
shadow into sunlit rooms, can never help

but break her secrecy again. Just listening
is a kind of guilt. The Westerkerk repeats
itself outside, as if all time worked round
towards her fear, and made each stroke die
down on guarded streets. Imagine it –

three years of whispering and loneliness
and plotting, day by day, the Allied line
in Europe with a yellow chalk. What hope
she had for ordinary love and interest
survives her here, displayed above the bed

as pictures of her family; some actors;
fashions chosen by Princess Elizabeth.
And those who stoop to see them find
not only patience missing its reward,
but one enduring wish for chances like

my own: to leave as simply as I do,
and walk where couples drift at ease
up dusty tree-lined avenues, or watch
a silent barge come clear of bridges
settling their reflections in the blue canal.

Andrew Motion

THE SINGING CAT

It was a little captive cat
    Upon a crowded train
His mistress takes him from his box
    To ease his fretful pain.

She holds him tight upon her knee
    The graceful animal
And all the people look at him
    He is so beautiful.

But oh he pricks and oh he prods
    And turns upon her knee
Then lifteth up his innocent voice
    In plaintive melody.

He lifteth up his innocent voice,
    He lifteth up, he singeth
And to each human countenance
    A smile of grace he bringeth.

He lifteth up his innocent paw
    Upon her breast he clingeth
And everybody cries, Behold
    The cat, the cat that singeth.

He lifteth up his innocent voice
    He lifteth up, he singeth
And all the people warm themselves
    In the love his beauty bringeth.

Stevie Smith

COMPOSED UPON WESTMINSTER BRIDGE

Earth has not anything to show more fair:
Dull would he be of soul who could pass by
A sight so touching in its majesty:
This City now doth like a garment wear
The beauty of the morning; silent, bare,
Ships, towers, domes, theatres, and temples lie
Open unto the fields, and to the sky;
All bright and glittering in the smokeless air.
Never did sun more beautifully steep
In his first splendour, valley, rock, or hill;
Ne'er saw I, never felt, a calm so deep!

The river glideth at his own sweet will:
Dear God! the very houses seem asleep;
And all that mighty heart is lying still!

William Wordsworth

ST LUKE

And it came to pass, that as he was praying in a certain place, when he ceased, one of his disciples said unto him, Lord, teach us to pray, as John also taught his disciples. And he said unto them, When ye pray, say, Our Father which art in heaven, Hallowed be thy name. Thy kingdom come. Thy will be done, as in heaven, so in earth. Give us day by day our daily bread. And forgive us our sins; for we also forgive every one that is indebted to us. And lead us not into temptation; but deliver us from evil. And he said unto them, Which of you shall have a friend, and shall go unto him at midnight, and say unto him, Friend, lend me three loaves; For a friend of mine in his journey is come to me, and I have nothing to set before him? And he from within shall answer and say, Trouble me not: the door is now shut, and my children are with me in bed; I cannot rise and give thee. I say unto you, Though he will not rise and give him because he is his friend, yet because of his importunity he will rise and give him as many as he needeth. And I say unto you, Ask, and it shall be given you; seek, and ye shall find; knock, and it shall be opened unto you. For every one that asketh receiveth; and he that seeketh findeth; and to him that knocketh it shall be opened.

THE WOMAN IN WHITE

I mounted the hill rapidly. The dark mass of the church-tower was the first object I discerned dimly against the night sky. As I turned aside to get round to the vestry, I heard heavy footsteps close to me. The servant had ascended to the church after us. 'I don't mean any harm,' he said, when I turned round on him, 'I'm only looking for my master.' The tones in which he spoke betrayed unmistakable fear. I took no notice of him and went on.

The instant I turned the corner and came in view of the vestry, I saw the lantern-skylight on the roof brilliantly lit up from within. It shone out with dazzling brightness against the murky, starless sky.

I hurried through the churchyard to the door.

As I got near there was a strange smell stealing out on the damp night air. I heard a snapping noise inside – I saw the light above grow brighter and brighter – a pane of the glass cracked – I ran to the door and put my hand on it. The vestry was on fire!

Before I could move, before I could draw my breath after that discovery, I was horror-struck by a heavy thump against the door from the inside. I heard the key worked violently in the lock – I heard a man's voice behind the door, raised to a dreadful shrillness, screaming for help.

The servant who had followed me staggered back shuddering, and dropped to his knees. 'Oh, my God!' he said, 'it's Sir Percival!'

Wilkie Collins

RING OF BRIGHT WATER

Travelling with otters is a very expensive business. There was now no question of again confining Mij to a box, and there is, unfortunately, no other legitimate means of carrying an otter by train. For the illegitimate means which I followed then and after, I paid, as do all who have recourse to black markets, highly. He travelled with me in a first-class sleeper, a form of transport which for some reason he enjoyed hugely; indeed from the very first he showed a perverse predilection for railway stations, and a total disregard for their deafening din and alarming crowd scenes.

At the barrier the railway official punched for me a dog ticket (on which I had noticed the words 'Give full Description') and had already turned to the next in the queue before his eyes widened in a perfect double take; then Mij was tugging up the crowded platform at the end of his lead, heedless of the shouts and the bustle, the screaming train hooters and rumbling luggage trolleys.

I had planned this operation with some care, visualizing each hazard and circumventing it as far as possible in advance; my hush money was already paid; the basket I carried contained everything conceivably necessary to Mij for the journey; over my left arm was an army blanket ready to protect the sheets from Mij's platform-grimed paws as soon as he entered the sleeper. When the initial penetration of the citadel, as it were, passed off without the slightest hitch, I felt that I had reaped no more than the just rewards of my forethought.

Gavin Maxwell

OF MICE AND MEN

It was quite dark now, but the fire lighted the trunks of the trees and the curving branches overhead. Lennie crawled slowly and cautiously around the fire until he was close to George. He sat back on his heels. George turned the bean-cans so that another side faced the fire. He pretended to be unaware of Lennie so close beside him.

'George,' very softly. No answer. 'George!'

'Whatta you want?'

'I was only foolin', George. I don't want no ketchup. I wouldn't eat no ketchup if it was right here beside me.'

'If it was here, you could have some.'

'But I wouldn't eat none, George. I'd leave it all for you. You could cover your beans with it and I wouldn't touch none of it.'

George still stared morosely at the fire. 'When I think of the swell time I could have without you, I go nuts. I never get no peace.'

Lennie still knelt. He looked off into the darkness across the river. 'George, you want I should go away and leave you alone?'

'Where the hell could you go?'

'Well I could. I could go off in the hills there. Some place I'd find a cave.'

'Yeah? How'd you eat. You ain't got sense enough to find nothing to eat.'

'I'd find things, George. I don't need no nice food with ketchup. I'd lay out in the sun and nobody'd hurt me. An' if I foun' a mouse, I could keep it. Nobody'd take it away from me.'

George looked quickly and searchingly at him. 'I been mean, ain't I?'

John Steinbeck

SAVILLE

It was from Mr Reagan that the idea sprang that Colin should sit for the examinations. The opportunity to go to the grammar school in the city came the following year, and if he failed the examination a second opportunity occurred the year after. If he failed again he would go to the secondary-modern school at the other end of the village, from which the pit recruited most of its miners.

'It's as Reagan says,' his father told them. 'Do you want him to be like me or like Reagan, getting paid for sitting on his backside all day? I know what I'd do.'

'Mr Reagan works,' his mother said. 'Sitting down is a different kind of work, that's all.'

'Ah, well,' his father said. 'You're the one that knows about education.' His mother, unlike his father, had stayed at school until she was fifteen. In a cupboard upstairs was a certificate carefully filled in with copper-plate script testifying to her efficiency at English, nature study and domestic science.

It was his father, however, who set him his homework, coming round the table whenever his mother had suggested some subject he might do, saying, 'He'll never learn nought from that,' taking the pencil and setting his own small, square hand, bruised, its nails blackened with coal, firmly in the middle of the paper and across the top, with much snorting and panting, printing in capital letters the subject of a composition: 'A FOOTBALL MATCH', 'SUNDAY SCHOOL', 'A RIDE ON A BUS'. Sometimes he would stand by the chair, waiting for him to start, stooping forward slightly to follow the words as he began, sometimes stepping back, whistling through his teeth until, finally, he called out, 'If you take all that time to begin, by God, the exam'll be over before you start.'

David Storey

LARK RISE TO CANDLEFORD

She found the hamlet unchanged every year; but, beyond the houses, everything had altered, for it was still summer when she went away and when she returned it was autumn. Along the hedgerows hips and haws and crab-apples were ripe and the ivory parchment flowers of the traveller's joy had become silver and silky. The last of the harvest had been carried and already the pale stubble was greening over. Soon the sheep would be turned into the fields to graze, then the ploughs would come and turn the earth brown once more.

At home, the plums on the front wall of the house were ripe and the warm, fruity smell of boiling jam drew all the wasps in the neighbourhood. Other jams, jellies, and pickles already stood on the pantry shelves. Big yellow vegetable marrows dangled from hooks, and ropes of onions and bunches of drying thyme and sage. The faggot pile was being replenished and the lamp was again lighted soon after tea.

For the first few days after her return the house would seem small and the hamlet bare, and she was inclined to give herself the airs of a returned traveller when telling of the places she had seen and the people she had met on her holiday. But that soon wore off and she slipped back into her own place again. The visits to Candleford were very pleasant and the conveniences of her cousins' home and their way of life had the charm of novelty; but the plain spotlessness of her own home, with few ornaments and no padding to obscure the homely outline, was good, too. She felt she belonged there.

Flora Thompson

'You must clothe that boy, Fortune, you must make him wear trousers and a tunic. And at night he must wear a night-shirt.'

So now, seeing that the idol was gone, Mr Fortune called Lueli into the hut and began to measure him. He had never learnt tailoring; however he supposed that by taking great care and doing his best he could turn out a suit of clothes which might insinuate the fact of their nakedness to the islanders of Fanua, even if it had no other merit. He measured Lueli, he wrote down the measurements, he made his calculations and drew a sort of ground plan. Then he fetched a roll of white cotton and having laid it upon the floor and tethered it with some books he crawled about on all fours cutting out the trousers and the tunic with a pair of nail-scissors; for he thought that the night-shirt might rest in abeyance for the present.

The nail-scissors could only manage very small bites, and by the time the cutting-out was completed he was rather dizzy and very hot from taking so much exercise on his knees. 'That will do for the present,' he thought, rolling up the pieces. 'This afternoon I will visit my parishioners.'

Sylvia Townsend Warner

SUMMER LIGHTNING

If anybody had told Hugo Carmody six months before that half-way through the following July he would be lurking in trysting-places like this, his whole being alert for the coming of a girl, he would have scoffed at the idea. He would have laughed lightly. Not that he had not been fond of girls. He had always liked girls. But they had been, as it were, the mere playthings, so to speak, of a financial giant's idle hour. Six months ago he had been the keen, iron-souled man of business, all his energies and thoughts devoted to the management of the Hot Spot.

But now he stood shuffling his feet and starting hopefully at every sound, while the leaden moments passed sluggishly on their way. Then his vigil was enlivened by a wasp, which stung him on the back of the hand. He was leaping to and fro, licking his wounds, when he perceived the girl of his dreams coming down the path.

'Ah!' cried Hugo.

He ceased to leap and, rushing forward, would have clasped her in a fond embrace. Many people advocate the old-fashioned blue-bag for wasp-stings, but Hugo preferred this treatment.

To his astonishment she drew back. And she was not a girl who usually drew back on these occasions.

'What's the matter?' he asked, pained. It seemed to him that a spanner had been bunged into a holy moment.

P. G. Wodehouse

'STOP ALL THE CLOCKS, CUT OFF THE TELEPHONE'

Stop all the clocks, cut off the telephone,
Prevent the dog from barking with a juicy bone,
Silence the pianos and with muffled drum
Bring out the coffin, let the mourners come.

Let aeroplanes circle moaning overhead
Scribbling on the sky the message He Is Dead,
Put the crêpe bows round the white necks of the public
    doves,
Let the traffic policemen wear black cotton gloves.

He was my North, my South, my East and West,
My working week and my Sunday rest,
My noon, my midnight, my talk, my song;
I thought that love would last for ever: I was wrong.

The stars are not wanted now: put out every one;
Pack up the moon and dismantle the sun;
Pour away the ocean and sweep up the wood.
For nothing now can ever come to any good.

W. H. Auden

EXERCISE BOOK

Two and two four
four and four eight
eight and eight sixteen . . .
Once again! says the master
Two and two four
four and four eight
eight and eight sixteen.

But look! the lyre bird
high on the wing
the child sees it
the child hears it
the child calls it
Save me
play with me
bird!
So the bird alights
and plays with the child
Two and two four . . .
Once again! says the master
and the child plays
and the bird plays too . . .
Four and four eight
eight and eight sixteen
and twice sixteen makes what?
Twice sixteen makes nothing
least of all thirty-two
anyhow
and off they go
For the child has hidden
The bird in his desk
and all the children
hear its song
and all the children
hear the music
and eight and eight in their turn
off they go
and four and four and two and two
in their turn fade away
and one and one make neither one nor two
but one by one off they go.
And the lyre-bird sings
and the child sings
and the master shouts
When you've quite finished playing the fool
But all the children
Are listening to the music
And the walls of the classroom
quietly crumble.

The window panes turn
once more to sand
the ink is sea
the desk is trees
the chalk is cliffs
and the quill pen
a bird again.

Paul Dehn

THE FOX

It was twenty years ago I saw the fox
Gliding along the edge of prickling corn,
A nefarious shadow
Between the emerald field and bristling hedge,
On velvet feet he went.

The wind was kind, withheld from him my scent
Till my threaded gaze unmasked him standing there,
The colour of last year's beech leaves, pointed black,
Poised, uncertain, quivering nose aware
Of danger throbbing through each licking leaf.
One foot uplifted, balanced on the brink
Of perennial fear, the hunter hunted stood.

I heard no alien stir in the friendly wood,
But the fox's sculpted attitude was tense
With scenting, listening, with a seventh sense
Flaring to the alert; I heard no sound
Threaten the morning; and followed his amber stare,
But in that hair-breadth moment, that flick of the eye,
He vanished.

And now, whenever I hear the expectant cry
Of hounds on the empty air,
I look to a gap in the hedge and see him there
Filling the space with fear; the trembling leaves
Are frozen in his stillness till I hear
His leashed-up breathing – how the stretch of time
Contracts within the flash of recreation!

Phoebe Hesketh

THE ENEMIES

Last night they came across the river and
Entered the city. Women were awake
With lights and food. They entertained the band,
Not asking what the men had come to take
Or what strange tongue they spoke
Or why they came so suddenly through the land.

Now in the morning all the town is filled
With stories of the swift and dark invasion;
The women say that not one stranger told
A reason for his coming. The intrusion
Was not for devastation:
Peace is apparent still on hearth and field.

Yet all the city is a haunted place.
Man meeting man speaks cautiously. Old friends
Close up the candid looks upon their face.
There is no warmth in hands accepting hands;
Each ponders, 'Better hide myself in case
Those strangers have set up their homes in minds
I used to walk in. Better draw the blinds
Even if the strangers haunt in my own house.'

Elizabeth Jennings

MR BLEANEY

'This was Mr Bleaney's room. He stayed
The whole time he was at the Bodies, till
They moved him.' Flowered curtains, thin and frayed,
Fall to within five inches of the sill,

Whose window shows a strip of building land,
Tussocky, littered. 'Mr Bleaney took
My bit of garden properly in hand.'
Bed, upright chair, sixty-watt bulb, no hook

Behind the door, no room for books or bags –
'I'll take it.' So it happens that I lie
Where Mr Bleaney lay, and stub my fags
On the same saucer-souvenir, and try

Stuffing my ears with cotton-wool, to drown
The jabbering set he egged her on to buy.
I know his habits – what time he came down,
His preference for sauce to gravy, why

He kept on plugging at the four aways –
Likewise their yearly frame: the Frinton folk
Who put him up for summer holidays,
And Christmas at his sister's house in Stoke.

But if he stood and watched the frigid wind
Tousling the clouds, lay on the fusty bed
Telling himself that this was home, and grinned,
And shivered, without shaking off the dread

That how we live measures our own nature,
And at his age having no more to show
Than one hired box should make him pretty sure
He warranted no better, I don't know.

Philip Larkin

CHRISTMAS LANDSCAPE

Tonight the wind gnaws
With teeth of glass,
The jackdaw shivers
in caged branches of iron,
the stars have talons.

There is hunger in the mouth
of vole and badger,
silver agonies of breath
in the nostril of the fox,
ice on the rabbit's paw.

Tonight has no moon,
no food for the pilgrim;
the fruit tree is bare,
the rose bush a thorn
and the ground bitter with stones.

But the mole sleeps, and the hedgehog
lies curled in a womb of leaves,
the bean and the wheat-seed
hug their germs in the earth
and the stream moves under the ice.

Tonight there is no moon,
but a new star opens
like a silver trumpet over the dead.
Tonight in a nest of ruins
the blessed babe is laid.

And the fir tree warms to a bloom of candles,
the child lights his lantern,
stares at his tinselled toy;
our hearts and hearths
smoulder with live ashes.

In the blood of our grief
the cold earth is suckled,
in our agony the womb
convulses its seed,
in the cry of anguish
the child's first breath is born.

Laurie Lee

SPRING

Nothing is so beautiful as spring –
  When weeds, in wheels, shoot long and lovely and
  lush;
  Thrush's eggs look little low heavens, and thrush
Through the echoing timber does so rinse and wring
The ear, it strikes like lightnings to hear him sing;

The glassy peartree leaves and blooms, they brush
   The descending blue; that blue is all in a rush
With richness; the racing lambs too have fair their fling.

What is all this juice and all this joy?
   A strain of the earth's sweet being in the beginning
In Eden garden. – Have, get, before it cloy,
   Before it cloud, Christ, lord, and sour with sinning,
Innocent mind and Mayday in girl and boy,
   Most, O maid's child, thy choice and worthy the
      winning.

                              Gerard Manley Hopkins

MY HAT

Mother said if I wore this hat
I should be certain to get off with the right sort of chap
Well look where I am now, on a desert island
With so far as I can see no one at all on hand
I know what has happened though I suppose Mother
      wouldn't see
This hat being so strong has completely run away with
      me
I had the feeling it was beginning to happen the moment
      I put it on
What a moment that was as I rose up, I rose up like a
      flying swan
As strong as a swan too, why see how far my hat has
      flown me away
It took us a night to come and then a night and a day
And all the time the swan wing in my hat waved
      beautifully
Ah, I thought, How this hat becomes me.
First the sea was dark but then it was pale blue
And still the wing beat and we flew and we flew
A night and a day and a night, and by the old right way
Between the sun and the moon we flew until morning
      day.
It is always early morning here on this peculiar island
The green grass grows into the sea on the dipping land

Am I glad I am here? Yes, well, I am,
It's nice to be rid of Father, Mother and the young man
There's just one thing causes me a twinge of pain,
If I take my hat off, shall I find myself home again?
So in this early morning land I always wear my hat
Go home, you see, well I wouldn't run a risk like that.

Stevie Smith

CORINTHIANS

Though I speak with the tongues of men and of angels, and have not charity, I am become as sounding brass, or a tinkling cymbal. And though I have the gift of prophecy, and understand all mysteries, and all knowledge; and though I have all faith, so that I could remove mountains, and have not charity, I am nothing. And though I bestow all my goods to feed the poor, and though I give my body to be burned, and have not charity, it profiteth me nothing. Charity suffereth long, and is kind: charity envieth not; charity vaunteth not itself, is not puffed up, Doth not behave itself unseemly, seeketh not her own, is not easily provoked, thinketh no evil; Rejoiceth not in iniquity, but rejoiceth in the truth; Beareth all things, believeth all things, hopeth all things, endureth all things. Charity never faileth: but whether there be prophecies, they shall fail; whether there be tongues, they shall cease; whether there be knowledge, it shall vanish away. For we know in part, and we prophesy in part. But when that which is perfect is come, then that which is in part shall be done away. When I was a child, I spake as a child, I understood as a child, I thought as a child; but when I became a man, I put away childish things. For now we see through a glass, darkly; but then face to face: now I know in part; but then shall I know even as also I am known. And now abideth faith, hope, charity, these three; but the greatest of these is charity.

The enormity of what he had done flooded back through her. She kept shaking her head. He went and took a chair and sat facing her, too far to touch, but close enough to appeal to her better self.

'Can you suppose for one serious moment that I am unpunished? That this has not been the most terrible decision of my life? This hour the most dreaded? The one I shall remember with the deepest remorse till the day I die? I may be – very well, I *am* a deceiver. But you know I am not heartless. I should not be here now if I were. I should have written a letter, fled abroad –'

'I wish you had.'

He gave the crown of her head a long look, then stood. He caught sight of himself in a mirror; and the man in the mirror. Charles in another world, seemed the true self. The one in the room was what she said, an impostor; had always been, in his relations with Ernestina, an impostor, an observed other. He went at last into one of his prepared speeches.

'I cannot expect you to feel anything but anger and resentment. All I ask is that when these . . . natural feelings have diminished you will recall that no condemnation of my conduct can approach the severity of my own . . . and that my one excuse is my incapacity longer to deceive a person whom I have learnt to respect and admire.'

It sounded false; it was false; and Charles was uncomfortably aware of her unpent contempt for him.

'I am trying to picture *her*. I suppose she is titled – has pretensions to birth. Oh . . . if I had only listened to my poor, dear father!'

'What does that mean?'

'He knows the nobility. He has a phrase for them – Fine manners and unpaid bills.'

'I am not a member of the nobility.'

'You are like your uncle. You behave as if your rank excuses you all concern with what we ordinary creatures of the world believe in. And so does she. What woman could be so vile as to make a man break his vows? I can guess.' She spat the guess out. 'She is married.'

John Fowles

All the evening Melbury had been coming to his door saying, 'I wonder where in the world that girl is! Never in all my born days did I know her bide out like this! She surely said she was going into the garden to get some parsley.'

Melbury searched the garden, the outbuildings, and the orchard, but could find no trace of her, and then he made inquiries at the cottages of such of his workmen as had not gone to bed, avoiding Tangs's because he knew the young people were to rise early to leave. In these inquiries one of the men's wives somewhat incautiously let out the fact that she had heard a scream in the wood, though from which direction she could not say.

This set Melbury's fears on end. He told the men to light lanterns, and headed by himself they started, Creedle following at the last moment with a bundle of grapnels and ropes which he could not be persuaded to leave behind, and the company being joined by the hollow-turner and Cawtree as they went along.

They explored the precincts of the village, and in a short time lighted upon the man-trap. Its discovery simply added an item of fact without helping their conjectures; but Melbury's indefinite alarm was greatly increased when, holding a candle to the ground, he saw in the teeth of the instrument some frayings from Grace's clothing. No intelligence of any kind was gained till they met a woodman of Delborough, who said that he had seen a lady answering to the description her father gave of Grace, walking through the wood on a gentleman's arm in the direction of Sherton.

'Was he supporting her?' said Melbury.

'Well – rather,' said the man.

'Did she walk lame?'

'Well, 'tis true her head hung over towards him a bit.'

Creedle groaned tragically.

Thomas Hardy

You got there by a slow boat, full of beatniks and Germans; and unless you were lucky you sat on the engine from which a reek of hot grease, coughed up by the pistons, accompanied the wallowing journey. It was six hours from Mallorca, empty sea all the way, and you dozed on a bed of rivets. That's how we got there anyway, knowing no other method. (They in fact built an airstrip during the course of our journey, but nobody told us about it.) So we idled all day across the hundred mile sea, playing dice and drinking bad wine, and when the island appeared at last in the twilight we felt we'd come to the end of the world.

I had no notion what to expect, I knew nothing about Ibiza and the young gentlemen from Palma in their blue dacron suits had coughed when I asked them about it. 'Very rough and brutish,' they said, 'very backward. No cars and no society.' And now it approached us – a red rock like a shell splinter, bare headlands like a new kind of metal, with a few bone-white temples standing on the empty shore among which a dark group of figures watched us.

It looked like a place no one else had visited, something waiting unused for this evening, the shade of some long-preserved netherworld even older than the Mediterranean. Who were these watchers among their temples? What were their clothes? their gods? We sidled nearer towards the quayside. Details grew steadily clearer. Revealing the watchers to be boys in more blue dacron suits, the temples new holiday bungalows; and we couldn't land till a French actress on board had been filmed disembarking three times . . .

Laurie Lee

STAYING ON

Tusker's mouth hung open. Her heart was racing, but triumphantly. She had never *stunned* him into silence. His silence now was like the silence she had years ago imagined creating in a darkened theatre, one which would hold until after her exit when it would be shattered by prolonged applause, a deserved ovation: the kind she had dreamed of and might have got back in 'Pindi before the war when they did *The Wind and the Rain*, except that that hard grasping little bitch Dulcie Thompson got the part, not that there'd ever been any doubt that she would nor that she, Lucy, would end up in the prompt-corner as assistant stage manager to the incompetent Captain Starling, and anyway the part had never been auditioned for. Leading parts went automatically to Dulcie and you took your life in your hands if you prompted her during one of her Pauses or alternatively got chewn to a rag if you couldn't tell the difference between a Pause and a Black-Out, which was virtually impossible because Dulcie's addiction to Pauses was matched only by her susceptibility to Black-Outs which she covered by succumbing to her other addiction – business: business with a handkerchief or a handbag, unrehearsed business that ruined other actors' concentration, even moving props that caused black-out for someone else a few minutes later when he found the prop not in its place.

'I need a prop now,' Lucy thought. 'Something to help me get off while Tusker's mouth is still open.' But there was no prop. She would have to ad lib.

Paul Scott

BARCHESTER TOWERS

She had got the better of Mr Slope, and she now thought well to show her husband that when allowed to get the better of everybody, when obeyed by him and permitted to rule over others, she would take care that he should have his reward. Mr Slope had not a chance against her; not only could she stun the poor bishop by her midnight anger, but she could assuage and soothe him, if she so willed, by daily indulgences. She could furnish his room for him, turn him out as smart a bishop as any on the bench, give him good dinners, warm fires, and an easy life; all this she would do if he would be quietly obedient. But if not –! To speak sooth, however, his sufferings on that dreadful night had been so poignant, as to leave him little spirit for further rebellion.

As soon as he had dressed himself she returned to his room. 'I hope you enjoyed yourself at —,' said she, seating herself on one side of the fire while he remained in his arm-chair on the other, stroking the calves of his legs. It was the first time he had had a fire in his room since the summer, and it pleased him; for the good bishop loved to be warm and cosy. Yes, he said, he had enjoyed himself very much. Nothing could be more polite than the archbishop; and Mrs Archbishop had been equally charming.

Mrs Proudie was delighted to hear it; nothing, she declared, pleased her so much as to think

> Her bairn respectit like the lave.

She did not put it precisely in these words, but what she said came to the same thing; and then, having petted and fondled her little man sufficiently, she proceeded to business.

'The poor dean is still alive,' said she.

'So I hear, so I hear,' said the bishop. 'I'll go to the deanery directly after breakfast to-morrow.'

'We are going to this party at Ullathorne to-morrow morning, my dear; we must be there early, you know – by twelve o'clock I suppose.'

'Oh – ah!' said the bishop; 'then I'll certainly call the next day.'

'Was much said about it at —?' asked Mrs Proudie.

'About what?' said the bishop.

'Filling up the dean's place,' said Mrs Proudie. As she spoke a spark of the wonted fire returned to her eye, and the bishop felt himself to be a little less comfortable than before.

Anthony Trollope

DEAR ME

The conflict was complicated by the intervention of Edith Evans, who reminded us all that it was a play with music, not an opera with dialogue. Immediately the musical contention between Austria and the Reich was forgotten. All fifteen bickering musicians were united against the muse of drama, or more accurately, against Edith Evans. As they filed out of the rehearsal hall to make way for the mummers, Professor Strietzel, carrying his violin case as though it contained a machine-gun, looked straight at poor Edith, and said with a wealth of sinister meaning, 'I don't know . . . how all zis . . . shall end!'

The play, performed in garrison theatres in very flimsy yet evocative sets, assuring a rapid continuity of action, opened in Salisbury, and was an instant success. One distinguished admiral was even compelled to admit to Edith Evans, 'By Jove, I'm embarrassed to say that this is the first play by Shakespeare I've seen since Richard of Bordeaux!'

One drawback of these garrison theatres was that there was no method of concealing the orchestra. Its members sat on the same level as the audience. It was merely the actors who were elevated. I noticed on the first night that the orchestra made use of a miniature chessboard in order to while away the time during the histrionics, and often musicians crept forward like troops in a dugout to make some snide move. As far as I could understand it was a permanent championship, Berlin versus Vienna.

I hoped and prayed that Edith Evans wouldn't notice what was going on, but on the fourth night, during a brilliant tirade, she stopped dead. One eye had alighted on the tiny chessboard just as an Austrian viola player had spotted a crack in the enemy defence, and was creeping forward on all fours to deliver the *coup de grâce*.

She faltered, fumbled, and then, with superb dramatic instinct, she looked at me and said, in a tone of pained surprise, 'What did you say?'

Peter Ustinov

TO THE LIGHTHOUSE

Nobody seemed to have spoken for an age. Cam was tired of looking at the sea. Little bits of black cork had floated past; the fish were dead in the bottom of the boat. Still her father read, and James looked at him and she looked at him, and they vowed that they would fight tyranny to the death, and he went on reading quite unconscious of what they thought.

It was thus that he escaped, she thought. Yes, with his great forehead and his great nose, holding his little mottled book firmly in front of him, he escaped. You might try to lay hands on him, but then like a bird, he spread his wings, he floated off to settle out of your reach somewhere far away on some desolate stump. She gazed at the immense expanse of the sea. The island had grown so small that it scarcely looked like a leaf any longer. It looked like the top of a rock which some big wave would cover. Yet in its frailty were all those paths, those terraces, those bedrooms – all those innumerable things. But as, just before sleep, things simplify themselves so that only one of all the myriad details has power to assert itself, so, she felt, looking drowsily at the island, all those paths and terraces and bedrooms were fading and disappearing, and nothing was left but a pale blue censer swinging rhythmically this way and that across her mind. It was a hanging garden; it was a valley, full of birds, and flowers, and antelopes . . . She was falling asleep.

'Come now,' said Mr Ramsay, suddenly shutting his book.

Come where? To what extraordinary adventure? She woke with a start. To land somewhere, to climb some-where? Where was he leading them? For after his immense silence the words startled them. But it was absurd. He was hungry, he said. It was time for lunch. Besides, look, he said. There's the Lighthouse. 'We're almost there.'

Virginia Woolf

————◆————

MUSÉE DES BEAUX ARTS

About suffering they were never wrong,
The Old Masters: how well they understood
Its human position; how it takes place
While someone else is eating or opening a window or
    just walking dully along;
How, when the aged are reverently, passionately waiting
For the miraculous birth, there always must be
Children who did not specially want it to happen, skating
On a pond at the edge of the wood:
They never forgot
That even the dreadful martyrdom must run its course
Anyhow in a corner, some untidy spot
Where the dogs go on with their doggy life and the
    torturer's horse
Scratches its innocent behind on a tree.
In Brueghel's Icarus, for instance: how everything turns
    away
Quite leisurely from the disaster; the ploughman may
Have heard the splash, the forsaken cry,
But for him it was not an important failure; the sun
    shone
As it had to on the white legs disappearing into the green
Water; and the expensive delicate ship that must have
    seen
Something amazing, a boy falling out of the sky,
Had somewhere to get to and sailed calmly on.

W. H. Auden

DIARY OF A CHURCH MOUSE

Here among long-discarded cassocks,
Damp stools, and half-split open hassocks,
Here where the Vicar never looks
I nibble through old service books.

Lean and alone I spend my days
Behind this Church of England baize.
I share my dark forgotten room
With two oil-lamps and half a broom.
The cleaner never bothers me,
So here I eat my frugal tea,
My bread is sawdust mixed with straw;
My jam is polish for the floor.
    Christmas and Easter may be feasts
For congregations and for priests,
And so may Whitsun. All the same,
They do not fill my meagre frame.
For me the only feast at all
Is Autumn's Harvest Festival,
When I can satisfy my want
With ears of corn around the font.
I climb the eagle's brazen head
To burrow through a loaf of bread.
I scramble up the pulpit stair
And gnaw the marrows hanging there.
    It is enjoyable to taste
These items ere they go to waste,
But how annoying when one finds
That other mice with pagan minds
Come into church my food to share
Who have no proper business there.
Two field mice who have no desire
To be baptized, invade the choir.
A large and most unfriendly rat
Comes in to see what we are at.
He says he thinks there is no God
And yet he comes . . . it's rather odd.
This year he stole a sheaf of wheat
(It screened our special preacher's seat),
And prosperous mice from fields away
Come in to hear the organ play,
And under cover of its notes
Ate through the altar's sheaf of oats.
A Low Church mouse, who thinks that I
Am too papistical, and High,

Yet somehow doesn't think it wrong
To munch through Harvest Evensong,
While I, who starve the whole year through,
Must share my food with rodents who
Except at this time of the year
Not once inside the church appear.
    Within the human world I know
Such goings-on could not be so,
For human beings only do
What their religion tells them to.
They read the Bible every day
And always, night and morning, pray,
And just like me, the good church mouse,
Worship each week in God's own house.
    But all the same it's strange to me
How very full the church can be
With people I don't see at all
Except at Harvest Festival.

John Betjeman

SLUG SONG

Consider the ubiquitous slug
be it snail, termite or bug
asking nothing save stalk or leaf
quite untroubled by metaphysic belief
inhabiting palaces of rock and river
sliding through life with sinuous quiver
minute lord of the plenteous earth
devouring it for all its diluvial worth.

By man's inveterate wrath subjected
to man's vast follies it stays unaffected
and I note yet another instance of its sagacity
wriggling along with such admirable tenacity;
however long it may have dawdled and tarried
I have yet to hear of a slug getting married
while I sit surrounded by manifold reminders
of what should have been eye-opening blinders

of what man's foolhardy supercilious estate
has wreaked on that most singular state
as I sadly contemplate my own crass contributions
to that enriching pluperfect of institutions.

And O joyous excellence of the humble slug —
it meanders through time without need of drug
crawling with sedate resolve to its destiny
undulating with serpentine zest and assiduity
and what matter if it fails to deduct or think —
certain it is that the slug does not drink
for who ever heard of bug, termite or worm
no matter how madly they shiver and squirm
in all manner of primordial esoteric dances
going into silly transcendental trances?

O how I envy snail, termite and slug
snug as God willed it in the proverbial rug
all petty guile lacking and unassuming
never once knowing what it is to be human.

Christy Brown

THE CANTERBURY TALES

This carpenter had married a young wife
Not long before, and loved her more than life.
She was a girl of eighteen years of age.
Jealous he was and kept her in the cage,
For he was old and she was wild and young;
He thought himself quite likely to be stung.
He might have known, were Cato on his shelf,
A man should marry someone like himself;
A man should pick an equal for his mate.
Youth and old age are often in debate.
His wits were dull, he'd fallen in the snare
And had to bear his cross as others bear.
She was a pretty creature, fair and tender,
And had a weasel's body, softly slender.
She used to wear a girdle of striped silk,

Her apron was as white as morning milk
To deck her loins, all gusseted and pleated.
Her smock was white; embroidery repeated
Its pattern on the collar front and back,
Inside and out; it was of silk, and black.
And all the ribbons on her milky mutch
Were made to match her collar, even such.
She wore a broad silk fillet rather high,
And certainly she had a lecherous eye.
And she had plucked her eyebrows into bows,
Slenderly arched they were, and black as sloes.
And a more truly blissful sight to see
She was than blossom on a cherry-tree,
And softer than the wool upon a wether.
And by her girdle hung a purse of leather,
Tasselled in silk, with metal droplets, pearled.
If you went seeking up and down the world
The wisest man you met would have to wrench
His fancy to imagine such a wench.
She had a shining colour, gaily tinted,
And brighter than a florin newly minted,
And when she sang it was as loud and quick
As any swallow perched above a rick.
And she would skip or play some game or other
Like any kid or calf behind its mother.
Her mouth was sweet as mead or honey – say
A hoard of apples lying in the hay
Skittish she was, and jolly as a colt,
Tall as a mast and upright as a bolt
Out of a bow. Her collaret revealed
A brooch as big as boss upon a shield
High shoes she wore, and laced them to the top.
She was a daisy, O a lollypop
For any nobleman to take to bed
Or some good man of yeoman stock to wed.

Geoffrey Chaucer

I KNEW YOU WITHOUT ENCHANTMENT

I knew you without enchantment
And for some years
We went our usual ways
Meeting occasionally
Finding no heights nor depths among our days
Shedding no tears
Every so often when we felt inclined
Living like lovers in each other's arms
Feeling no qualms
In our light intimacy
So resolute we were in heart and mind
So steeled against illusion, deaf and blind
To all presentiment, to all enchantment
(I knew you without enchantment).

It is so strange
Remembering that phase
Those unexacting, uneventful days
Before the change
Before we knew this serio-comic, tragic
Most unexpected, overwhelming magic.
I knew you without enchantment.

And to-day I cannot think of you without my heart
Suddenly stopping
Or, in those long grey hours we spent apart
Dropping, dropping
Down into desolation like a stone.
To be alone
No longer means to me clear time and space
In which to stretch my mind.

I see your face
Between me and the space I used to find
Between me and the other worlds I seek
There stands your sleek
And most beloved silhouette
And yet
I can remember not so long ago

We neither of us cared
Nor dared
To know
How swiftly we were nearing the abyss
(This foolish, quite ungovernable bliss)
Let's not regret
That empty life before. It was great fun
And hurt no one
There was no harm in it
At certain moments there was even charm in it.

But oh my dearest love, there was no spell
No singing heaven and no wailing hell.
I knew you without enchantment.

Noël Coward

WARNING TO CHILDREN

Children, if you dare to think
Of the greatness, rareness, muchness,
Fewness of this precious only
Endless world in which you say
You live, you think of things like this:
Blocks of slate enclosing dappled
Red and green, enclosing tawny
Yellow nets, enclosing white
And black acres of dominoes,
Where a neat brown paper parcel
Tempts you to untie the string.
In the parcel a small island,
On the island a large tree,
On the tree a husky fruit.
Strip the husk and pare the rind off:
In the kernel you will see
Blocks of slate enclosed by dappled
Red and green, enclosed by tawny
Yellow nets, enclosed by white
And black acres of dominoes,

Where the same brown paper parcel –
Children, leave the string alone!
For who dares undo the parcel
Finds himself at once inside it,
On the island, in the fruit,
Blocks of slate about his head,

Finds himself enclosed by dappled
Green and red, enclosed by yellow
Tawny nets, enclosed by black
And white acres of dominoes,
With the same brown paper parcel
Still unopened on his knee.
And, if he then should dare to think
Of the fewness, muchness, rareness,
Greatness of this endless only
Precious world in which he says
He lives – he then unties the string.

Robert Graves

THE PIANO

Somewhere beneath that piano's superb sleek black
Must hide my mother's piano, little and brown, with the
    back
That stood close to the wall, and the front's faded silk,
    both torn,
And the keys with little hollows, that my mother's
    fingers had worn.

Softly, in the shadows, a woman is singing to me
Quietly, through the years I have crept back to see
A child sitting under the piano, in the boom of the
    shaking strings
Pressing the little poised feet of the mother who smiles as
    she sings.

The full throated woman has chosen a winning, living
   song
And surely the heart that is in me must belong
To the old Sunday evenings, when darkness wandered
   outside
And hymns gleamed on our warm lips, as we watched
   mother's fingers glide.

Or this is my sister at home in the old front room
Singing love's first surprised gladness, alone in the
   gloom.
She will start when she sees me, and blushing, spread out
   her hands
To cover my mouth's raillery, till I'm bound in her
   shame's heartspun bands.

A woman is singing me a wild Hungarian air
And her arms, and her bosom, and the whole of her soul
   is bare,
And the great black piano is clamouring as my mother's
   never could clamour
And my mother's tunes are devoured of this music's
   ravaging glamour.

                                        D. H. Lawrence

THE ALBUM

I see you, a child
In a garden sheltered for buds and playtime,
Listening as if beguiled
By a fancy beyond your years and the flowering
   maytime.
The print is faded: soon there will be
No trace of that pose enthralling,
Nor visible echo of my voice distantly calling
'Wait! Wait for me!'

Then I turn the page
To a girl who stands like a questioning iris
By the waterside, at an age
That asks every mirror to tell what the heart's desire is.
The answer she finds in that oracle stream
Only time could affirm or disprove,
Yet I wish I was there to venture a warning, 'Love
Is not what you dream.'

Next you appear
As if garlands of wild felicity crowned you
Courted, caressed, you wear
Like immortelles the lovers and friends around you.
'They will not last you, rain or shine,
They are but straws and shadows,'
I cry: 'Give not to those charming desperadoes
What was made to be mine.'

One picture is missing
The last. It would show me a tree stripped bare
By intemperate gales, her amazing
Noonday of blossom spoilt which promised so fair.
Yet, scanning those scenes at your heyday taken,
I tremble, as one who must view
In the crystal a doom he could never deflect – yes, I too
Am fruitlessly shaken.

I close the book;
But the past slides out of its leaves to haunt me
And it seems, wherever I look,
Phantoms of irreclaimable happiness taunt me.
Then I see her, petalled in new-blown hours,
Beside me – 'All you love most there
Has blossomed again,' she murmurs, 'all that you missed
     there
Has grown to be yours.'

                                        C. Day Lewis

My one and only meeting with Dylan Thomas occurred in the Swiss Cottage pub. I sat at a table, on my own, when Dylan Thomas came in with a companion. His friend edged towards the bar and Dylan himself, looking like his photograph, made for my table. At that time I was full of admiration for his poetry. Many of the poems that were soon to be collected in *Deaths and Entrances* had been given an airing in the literary magazines, *Horizon, Life and Letters*, etc. and I had been spellbound by them. As he settled himself in the chair next to me I grew hysterical in my silence. I wanted somehow to say that I liked his poetry; on the other hand I did not wish to presume and certainly I did not want my mouth to be full of soap. Finally, I ventured timidly, 'You're Dylan Thomas.' He turned his head, surprised. 'I think you know my cousin, Leo Solomon, from Swansea,' I added quickly.

'Who?'

'Leo Solomon.'

Dylan Thomas seemed puzzled. My cousin had told me that he knew Dylan well, that they were old buddies, that he had taken Dylan back many a time to my uncle's, his father's house. *Didn't Leo Solomon even know Dylan Thomas's dreams?*

'Leo Solomon, the painter,' I said, desperately.

Dylan Thomas hardly reacted. He seemed shy and preoccupied. His friend at the bar was having difficulty in drawing the barmaid's attention. I began to wish that I had not spoken, that I had not blundered so familiarly. It was too late now. 'Leo Solomon . . . my cousin . . . the painter . . . from Swansea,' I insisted. I had spoken very slowly with great deliberation and I hoped Dylan Thomas did not think I was treating him as a moron, or as one deaf who needed to lip-read.

'Yes,' said Dylan Thomas at last, and he looked around furtively, obviously wanting to get away.

Embarrassed, I thought it best to quit. After a decent interval of one and a half minutes, I finished off the half pint of the beer I had been half-drinking and rose. 'Bye,' I said to Dylan Thomas. He half smiled. He also half rose with deep courtesy and said, 'Bye, Mr Solomon.'

Naturally I wanted to tell him my real name. My name is Dannie Abse, the ego-clamour in me wanted to cry, and I write poetry too! I said nothing, of course.

Dannie Abse

ST LUKE

And, behold, two of them went that same day to a village called Emmaus, which was from Jerusalem about threescore furlongs. And they talked together of all these things which had happened. And it came to pass, that, while they communed together and reasoned, Jesus himself drew near, and went with them. But their eyes were holden that they should not know him. And he said unto them, What manner of communications are these that ye have one to another, as ye walk, and are sad? And the one of them, whose name was Cleopas, answering said unto him, Art thou only a stranger in Jerusalem, and hast not known the things which are come to pass there in these days? And he said unto them, What things? And they said unto him, Concerning Jesus of Nazareth, which was a prophet mighty in deed and word before God and all the people: And how the chief priests and our rulers delivered him to be condemned to death, and have crucified him. But we trusted that it had been he which should have redeemed Israel: and beside all this, to day is the third day since these things were done. Yea, and certain women also of our company made us astonished, which were early at the sepulchre; And when they found not his body, they came, saying, that they had also seen a vision of angels, which said that he was alive. And certain of them which were with us went to the sepulchre, and found it even so as the women had said: but him they saw not. Then he said unto them, O fools, and slow of heart to believe all that the prophets have spoken: Ought not Christ to have suffered these things, and to enter into his glory? And beginning at Moses and all the prophets, he expounded unto them in all the scriptures the things concerning himself. And they drew nigh unto the village, whither they went: and he made as though he would have gone further. But they constrained him, saying, Abide with us: for it is toward evening, and the day is far spent. And he went in to tarry with them. And it came to pass, as he sat at meat with them, he took bread, and blessed it, and brake, and gave to them. And their eyes were opened, and they knew him; and he vanished out of their sight. And they said one to another, Did not our heart burn within us, while he talked with us by the way, and while he opened to us the scriptures? And they rose up the same hour, and returned to Jerusalem, and found the eleven gathered together, and them that were with them, Saying, The Lord is risen indeed, and hath appeared to Simon. And they told what things were done in the way, and how he was known of them in breaking of bread.

HATTER'S CASTLE

As Denis sat alone, in the silent, cabined space of his compartment, tossed this way and that by the jactation, he felt suddenly that the grinding wheels of the train spoke to him. As they raced upon the line he heard them rasp out, with a heavy, despairing refrain: 'God help us! God help us! God help us!'

Amidst the blare of the storm this slow, melancholy dirge beat itself into Denis' brain. The certain sense of some terrible disaster began to oppress him. Strangely, he feared not for himself, but for Mary. Frightful visions flashed through the dark field of his imagination. He saw her, in a white shroud, with sad, imploring eyes, with dank, streaming hair, with bleeding feet and hands. Fantastic shapes oppressed her which made her shrink into the obliterating darkness. Again he saw her grimacing, simpering palely like a sorry statue of the Madonna and holding by the hand the weazened figure of a child. He shouted in horror. In a panic of distress he jumped to his feet. He desired to get to her. He wanted to open the door, to jump out of this confining box which enclosed him like a sepulchre. He would have given, instantly, everything he possessed to get out of the train. But he could not.

He was imprisoned in the train, which advanced inexorably, winding in its own glare like a dark, red serpent twisting sinuously forward. It had traversed one mile of the bridge and had now reached the middle span, where a mesh of steel girders formed a hollow tube through which it must pass. The train entered this tunnel. It entered slowly, fearfully, reluctantly, juddering in every bolt and rivet of its frame as the hurricane assaulted, and sought to destroy, the greater resistance now offered to it. The wheels clanked with the ceaseless insistence of the tolling of a passing-bell, still protesting, endlessly: 'God help us! God help us! God help us!'

Then, abruptly, when the whole train lay enwrapped within the iron lamellæ of the middle link of the bridge, the wind elevated itself with a culminating, exultant roar to the orgasm of its power and passion.

The bridge broke. Steel girders snapped like twigs, cement crumbled like sand, iron pillars bent like willow wands. The middle span melted like wax. Its wreckage clung around the tortured train, which gyrated madly for an instant in space. Immediately, a shattering rush of broken glass and wood descended upon Denis, cutting and bruising him with mangling violence. He felt the wrenching torsion of metal, and the grating of falling masonry. The inexpressible desolation of a hundred human voices, united in a sudden, short anguished cry of mingled agony and terror, fell upon his ears hideously, with the deathly fatality of a coronach. The walls of his compartment whirled about him and upon him, like a winding-sheet, the floor rushed over his head. As he spun round, with a loud cry he, too, shouted: 'God help us!' then, faintly, the name: 'Mary!'

Then the train with incredible speed, curving like a rocket, arched the darkness in a glittering parabola of light, and plunged soundlessly into the black hell of water below, where, like a rocket, it was instantly extinguished – for ever obliterated! For the infinity of a second, as he hurtled through the air, Denis knew what had happened. He knew everything, then instantly he ceased to know. At the same instant as the first, faint cry of his child ascended feebly in the byre at Levenford, his mutilated body hit the dark, raging water and lay dead, deep down upon the bed of the firth.

A. J. Cronin

THE PICKWICK PAPERS

From the centre of the ceiling of this kitchen, old Wardle had just suspended, with his own hands, a huge branch of mistletoe, and this same branch of mistletoe instantaneously gave rise to a scene of general and delightful struggling and confusion; in the midst of which, Mr Pickwick, with a gallantry that would have done honour to a descendant of Lady Tollimglower herself, took the old lady by the hand, led her beneath the mystic branch, and saluted her in all courtesy and decorum. The old lady submitted to this piece of practical politeness with all the dignity which befitted so important and serious a solemnity, but the younger ladies, not being so thoroughly imbued with a superstitious veneration for the custom; or imagining that the value of a salute is very much enhanced if it cost a little trouble to obtain it: screamed and struggled, and ran into corners, and threatened and remonstrated, and did everything but leave the room, until some of the less adventurous gentlemen were on the point of desisting, when they all at once found it useless to resist any longer, and submitted to be kissed with a good grace. Mr Winkle kissed the young lady with the black eyes, and Mr Snodgrass kissed Emily, and Mr Weller, not being particular about the form of being under the mistletoe, kissed Emma and the other female servants, just as he caught them. As to the poor relations, they kissed everybody, not even excepting the plainer portions of the young-lady visitors, who, in their excessive confusion, ran right under the mistletoe, as soon as it was hung up, without knowing it! Wardle stood with his back to the fire, surveying the whole scene, with the utmost satisfaction; and the fat boy took the opportunity of appropriating to his own use, and summarily devouring, a particularly fine mince-pie, that had been carefully put by for somebody else.

Charles Dickens

Now let me describe what actually happened to me at the Opera. Not only was I in evening dress by compulsion, but I voluntarily added many graces of conduct as to which the management made no stipulation whatever. I was in my seat in time for the first chord of the overture. I did not chatter during the music nor raise my voice when the Opera was too loud for normal conversation. I did not get up and go out when the statue music began. My language was fairly moderate considering the number and nature of the improvements on Mozart volunteered by Signor Caruso, and the respectful ignorance of the dramatic points of the score exhibited by the conductor and the stage manager – if there is such a functionary at Covent Garden. In short, my behaviour was exemplary.

At 9 o'clock (the Opera began at 8) a lady came in and sat down very conspicuously in my line of sight. She remained there until the beginning of the last act. I do not complain of her coming late and going early; on the contrary, I wish she had come later and gone earlier. For this lady, who had very black hair, had stuck over her right ear the pitiable corpse of a large white bird, which looked exactly as if someone had killed it by stamping on its breast, and then nailed it to the lady's temple, which was presumably of sufficient solidity to bear the operation. I am not, I hope, a morbidly squeamish person, but the spectacle sickened me. I presume that if I had presented myself at the doors with a dead snake round my neck, a collection of blackbeetles pinned to my shirtfront, and a grouse in my hair, I should have been refused admission. Why, then is a woman to be allowed to commit such a public outrage? Had the lady been refused admission, as she should have been, she would have soundly rated the tradesman who imposed the disgusting headdress on her under the false pretence that 'the best people' wear such things, and withdrawn her custom from him; and thus the root of the evil would be struck at; for your fashionable woman generally allows herself to be dressed according to the taste of a person whom she would not let sit down in her presence. I once, in Drury Lane Theatre, sat behind a *matinee* hat decorated with the two wings of a seagull, artificially reddened at the joints so as to produce the illusion of being freshly plucked from a live bird. But even that lady stopped short of the whole seagull. Both ladies were evidently regarded by their neighbours as ridiculous and vulgar; but that is hardly enough when the offence is one which produces a sensation of physical sickness in persons of normal humane sensibility.

I suggest to the Covent Garden authorities that, if they feel bound to protect their subscribers against the danger of my shocking them with a blue tie, they are at least equally bound to protect me against the danger of a woman shocking me with a dead bird.

Bernard Shaw

AT SCHOOL

I take it that to judge well is one of the purposes of education, and how can you judge well if you are not grounded in the classics? Well – that is how they thought at my school. There we studied only the classics of our language, the good poems and the bad-good poems, alike honoured by Time. As our English mistress read the poems aloud to us, a line would strike across to me, a story grip, a picture take colour. I liked grand words and story poems. I liked 'Arethusa arose from her couch of snows, in the Acroceraunian mountains' (the first poem I learnt by heart) for its grand words. And – of course – best of all the story-picture poems I liked 'The Ancient Mariner' . . . tasting the salt on my blackened lips . . . panting for rain . . . seeing for ever and ever the sea creatures twining for their pleasure. It was their inhumanity I loved. Away from school we had our nursery rhymes, and – in the *Playbox Annual* I remember – a rhymed alphabet very dear to me, 'Admiral A., Blithe and gay, In a paper boat, He sailed away.' We learnt a lot by heart at my school, for homework, and also as a penalty if we broke rules. This, far from putting one off, put one on (at least so I found) and as sometimes, when we got older, it had to be Latin, I acquired a good deal of Catullus – '*Paeninsularum Sirmio insularumque*' – along with Tennyson's 'Ulysses', some Milton ('Me worse than wet thou findst not' seemed to me awfully funny. Well, I think it is) and Browning's 'Childe Roland to the Dark Tower Came'. How that repulsive horse . . . 'thrust out past service from the devil's stud' does stick in the mind, the whole poem was for me a landscape of Passchendaele. I also liked and liked to declaim 'The Solitude of Alexander Selkirk' . . . 'I am lord of the fowl and the brute' and certain picked lines with malice intent: 'In pride of power and beauty's bloom, Had wept o'er Monmouth's bloody tomb' ('Please, Miss Donovan' – our English mistress – 'what was he doing so far north, did she mean Montrose?') And Dryden's ever-useful: 'When parents their commands unjustly lay, Children are privileged to disobey.' I think it is a good thing for children to be made to learn by heart, most of them do it pretty easily anyway, then later, thinking about the poems and saying them over, one finds they stretch out and take fresh meanings – not always, I dare say, what the poets intended.

Stevie Smith

A QUIET YEAR

When Christmas is over and the New Year, a restful time begins at Minack. We are waiting for the daffodils, we have time on our own, and in January Cornwall belongs to its residents and for them it becomes like a huge garden. Roads are free of drivers who think they are still on motorways, carparks are free of attendants, beaches are empty for gulls and other seabirds, one can walk for miles on the coastal path without seeing anyone coming towards you, and while one reads accounts of a harsh winter elsewhere, one rejoices in the dawning of spring. Courting ravens grunt at each other, coltsfoot perfumes the bank of a stream, a sudden primrose shines in a meadow and spikes of early daffodils show above ground. One is aware that the world is beginning again, not the Man-made world but the world of Creation. It is a slow world which one watches. One has to have patience to see it, and feel it. It is the feeling of it which enriches the soul. Anyone can *see* the countryside. The lucky ones are those who have the time to be absorbed by it.

I could not, however, have been a countryman all my life. I had to experience the city life of rushing for trains, queuing for buses, being anxious about my job and, for that matter, living at times a life of elegant sophistication. Jeannie and I had done all these things and, like so many others, there arrived a moment in our lives when we knew we had to break away.

We still return though, still from time to time experience again the life we have left. We enjoy ourselves, but part of that enjoyment is the knowledge that we will only be away for three or four days. Indeed it is my custom to say to Jeannie when we set off for London, luggage in the back of the Volvo, slowly going over Monty's Leap, then on up the winding lane . . . it is my custom to say to Jeannie: 'Now that we have started, we are already on the way back here!'

Derek Tangye

DUCHESS AND THE JEWELLER

'And today, Duchess – what can I do for you today?' said Oliver, very softly.

The Duchess opened her heart, her private heart, gaped wide. And with a sigh but no words she took from her bag a long washleather pouch – it looked like a lean yellow ferret. And from a slit in the ferret's belly she dropped pearls – ten pearls. They rolled from the slit in the ferret's belly – one, two, three, four – like the eggs of some heavenly bird.

'All's that's left me, dear Mr Bacon,' she moaned. Five, six, seven – down they rolled, down the slopes of the vast mountain sides that fell between her knees into one narrow valley – the eighth, the ninth, and the tenth. There they lay in the glow of the peach-blossom taffeta. Ten pearls.

'From the Appleby cincture,' she mourned. 'The last . . . the last of them all.'

Oliver stretched out and took one of the pearls between finger and thumb. It was round, it was lustrous. But real was it, or false? Was she lying again? Did she dare?

128

She laid her plump padded finger across her lips. 'If the Duke knew . . .' she whispered. 'Dear Mr Bacon, a bit of bad luck . . .'

Been gambling again, had she?

'That villain! That sharper!' she hissed.

The man with the chipped cheek bone? A bad 'un. And the Duke was straight as a poker; with side whiskers; would cut her off, shut her up down there if he knew – what I know, thought Oliver, and glanced at the safe.

'Araminta, Daphne, Diana,' she moaned. 'It's for *them*.'

The ladies Araminta, Daphne, Diana – her daughters. He knew them; adored them. But it was Diana he loved.

'You have all my secrets,' she leered. Tears slid; tears fell; tears, like diamonds, collecting powder in the ruts of her cherry blossom cheeks.

'Old friend,' she murmured, 'old friend.'

'Old friend,' he repeated, 'old friend,' as if he licked the words.

'How much?' he queried.

She covered the pearls with her hand.

'Twenty thousand,' she whispered.

Virginia Woolf

THE SCHOLAR SPEAKS, IN HER RETIREMENT

I once had tea with Otto Jespersen.
We had been in correspondence. Things
In the manuscript of *Beowulf*
(Cotton Vitellius) I saw as pointers
To readings in the Middle-English *Pearl*.
I was a graduate student then, a girl.

I called, naturally it was at his
Suggestion, one late summer afternoon
At his country home in Western Denmark,
Walking from the station. He was most
Welcoming. He cut a dark brown cake.
Later he took me rowing on the lake.

His arms were sinewy, curiously brown,
I thought, for a scholar's, I don't know why; eyes
Of distinct blue. We travelled smoothly
In hot light. I felt I should have had
A parasol. The sun, starting to die,
Recklessly oranged almost half the sky.

He paid delicate compliments to my
Scholarship. The oars were entering in
And lifting, entering in again,
Dripping crystals of light. The water
Rolled back like silk sheets. Still,
It was all so still, round our boat's small turmoil.

I left him late, almost at nightfall. My head
Was turning with the stimulus of talk.
Any philologist would have envied me;
To be received by Jespersen, and shown
Such courtesy. He walked me to the train,
And shook hands. We did not meet again.

Across the half a century of my own
Modest achievement, I have held those hours
And those colours, the blues, the browns, the
clean
Unfolding waters. All my researches were
A rediscovering at whatever cost
Of what I found there; or of what I lost.

John Cassidy

DIGGING

Between my finger and my thumb
The squat pen rests; snug as a gun.

Under my window, a clean rasping sound
When the spade sinks into gravelly ground:
My father, digging. I look down

Till his straining rump among the flowerbeds
Bends low, comes up twenty years away
Stooping in rhythm through potato drills
Where he was digging.

The coarse boot nestled on the lug, the shaft
Against the inside knee was levered firmly.
He rooted out tall tops, buried the bright edge deep
To scatter new potatoes that we picked
Loving their cool hardness in our hands.

By God, the old man could handle a spade.
Just like his old man.

My grandfather cut more turf in a day
Than any other man on Toner's bog.
Once I carried him milk in a bottle
Corked sloppily with paper. He straightened up
To drink it, then fell to right away
Nicking and slicing neatly, heaving sods
Over his shoulder, going down and down
For the good turf. Digging.

The cold smell of potato mould, the squelch and slap
Of soggy peat, the curt cuts of an edge
Through living roots awaken in my head.
But I've no spade to follow men like them.

Between my finger and my thumb
The squat pen rests.
I'll dig with it.

Seamus Heaney

EARTHQUAKE

An old man's flamingo-coloured kite
Twitches higher over tiled roofs.
Idly gazing through the metal gauze
That nets the winter sun beyond my sliding windows,
I notice that all the telegraph-poles along the lane
Are waggling convulsively, and the wires
Bounce like skipping-ropes round flustered birds.
The earth creeps under the floor. A cherry tree
Agitates itself outside, but it is no wind
That makes the long bamboo palisade
Begin to undulate down all its length.

The clock stammers and stops. There is a queer racket,
Like someone rapping on the wooden walls,
Then through the ceilings's falling flakes I see
The brass handles on a high chest of drawers
Dithering and dancing in a brisk distraction.
The lamp swings like a headache, and the whole house
Rotates slightly on grinding rollers.
Smoothly, like a spoilt child putting out a tongue,
A drawer shoots half-out, and quietly glides back again,
Closed with a snap of teeth, a sharper click
Than such a casual grimace prepared me for.

The stove-pipe's awkward elbow
Twangles its three supporting wires. Doors
Slam, fly open: my quiet maid erupts from

Nowhere, blushing furiously, yet smiling wildly
As if to explain, excuse, console and warn.
Together, like lost children in a fairy-tale
Who escape from an enchanter's evil cottage,
We rush out into the slightly unbalanced garden. A pole
Vibrates still like a plucked bass string,
But the ground no longer squirms beneath our feet,
And the trees are composing themselves, have birds
    again.

In the spooky quiet, a 'plane drones
Like a metal top, and though the sound
Gives a sense of disaster averted,
And is even oddly re-assuring, as
The pulse of confident engines,
Throbbing high above an electric storm, can comfort,
We feel that somewhere out of sight
Something has done its worst. Meanwhile,
The house tries to look as if nothing had happened,
And over the roof's subtle curves
Lets the flamingo-coloured kite fly undisturbed.

James Kirkup

ALL DAY IT HAS RAINED . . .

All day it has rained, and we on the edge of the moors
Have sprawled in our bell-tents, moody and dull as
    boors,
Groundsheets and blankets spread on the muddy ground
And from the first grey wakening we have found
No refuge from the skirmishing fine rain
And the wind that made the canvas heave and flap
And the taut wet guy-ropes ravel out and snap.
All day the rain has glided, wave and mist and dream,
Drenching the gorse and heather, a gossamer stream
Too light to stir the acorns that suddenly
Snatched from their cups by the wild south-westerly
Pattered against the tent and our upturned dreaming
    faces.

And we stretched out, unbuttoning our braces,
Smoking a Woodbine, darning dirty socks,
Reading the Sunday papers – I saw a fox
And mentioned it in the note I scribbled home; –
And we talked of girls, and dropping bombs on Rome,
And thought of the quiet dead and the loud celebrities
Exhorting us to slaughter, and the herded refugees;
– Yet thought softly, morosely of them, and as
    indifferently
As of ourselves or those whom we
For years have loved, and will again
Tomorrow maybe love; but now it is the rain
Possesses us entirely, the twilight and the rain.

And I can remember nothing dearer or more to my heart
Than the children I watched in the woods on Saturday
Shaking down burning chestnuts for the schoolyard's
    merry play,
Or the shaggy patient dog who followed me
By Sheet and Steep and up the wooded scree
To the Shoulder o' Mutton where Edward Thomas
    brooded long
On death and beauty – till a bullet stopped his song.

Alun Lewis

GOOD DREAM

He woke in his usual room, decided
Feeling completely awake to switch
The reading lamp on and read – but where
Is the switch? No switch no light. No light
No chapter nor verse. Completely awake
He gropes for the switch and finds the book
He left in the dark but what is a book
Left in the dark? He feels the book
Suddenly gently taken away
By someone's hand and a warm voice
Begins, beginneth, aloud in the dark:
Here beginneth the first chapter –
But it wasn't the first, he was half way through.

No, says the voice, *the first chapter*
At the first verse in the first voice,
Which is mine, none other's: Here beginneth –
But I tell you, he says, I was half way through,
I am completely awake, I can prove it;
Where is the switch? I will show you the place
Half way through.
　　　　　　　　There is no switch,
The voice replies; *in the beginning*
Is darkness upon the face of the earth
In which you must wait for me till I
Show you the place not half way through
But just begun, the place your never
Knew was here.
　　　　　　　　But I know this place,
It is my usual room, except
The switch has gone.
　　　　　　　　The switch was never
There to start with; which is why
You refuse to wake.
　　　　　　　　But I am completely
Awake, I told you.
　　　　　　　　You will tell me
Once you are. Here beginneth –
I tell you this is my usual room;
I can put out my hand from the bed and feel the . . .
Yes?
　　The wall – but I can't. Where
Has the wall gone? My bed was against it.
What was against it?
　　　　　　　　Why is your voice
Moving away? Why do I hear
Water over it?
　　　　　　　　There is water
Between us, I am here on the bank,
You will have to row.
　　　　　　　　Row?
　　　　　　　　　　What
Is a boat for? I am here on the bank.
But I need light to row.
　　　　　　　　No.

No light until you reach this bank.
Feel for your oars.
                             Here are my oars.
Then loose that rope. Are you ready? Row.
Here beginneth . . .
                             He dips his oars
And knows the walls receding, hears
The ripples round the chair legs, hears
Larksong high in the chimney, hears
Rustling leaves in the wardrobe, smells
All the smells of a river, and yet
Feeling, smelling, hearing, knowing,
Still cannot see. This boat has no
Switch. No switch no light.
                             No light?
Pull on your oars. I am here.
                             He pulls.
Splutter of water, crackle and grinding
Of reeds and twigs; then bump. The hand
That stole the book that was left in the dark
Comes out of the dark, the hand that is hers,
Hers, none other's, and seizes his
To help him on to the bank.
                             'And God
Said Let there be light.'
                             His usual room
Has lost its usual walls and found
Four walls of sky, incredible blue
Enclosing incredible green enclosing
Her, none other.
                             Completely awake.

                             Louis MacNeice

THE POT GERANIUM

Green slated gables clasp the stem of the hill
In the lemony autumn sun; an acid wind
Dissolves the leaf-stalks of back-garden trees,

And chimneys with their fires unlit
Seem yet to puff a yellow smoke of poplars.
Freestone is brown as bark, and the model bakery
That once was a Primitive Methodist Chapel
Lifts its cornice against the sky.
And now, like a flight of racing pigeons
Slipped from their basket in the station yard,
A box-kite rides the air, a square of calico,
Crimson as the cornets of the Royal Temperance Band
When they brass up the wind in marching. The kite
Strains and struggles on its leash, and unseen boys,
In chicken run or allotment or by the side
Of the old quarry full to the gullet with water,
Pay out on their string a rag of dream,
High as the Jubilee flagpole.
                              I turn from the window
(Letting the bobbins of autumn wind up the swallows)
And lie on my bed. The ceiling
Slopes over like a tent, and white walls
Wrap themselves round me, leaving only
A flap for the light to blow through. Thighs and spine
Are clamped to the mattress and looping springs
Twine round my chest and hold me. I feel the air
Move on my face like spiders, see the light
Slide across the plaster; but wind and sun
Are mine no longer, nor have I kite to claim them,
Or string to fish the clouds. But there on a shelf
In the warm corner of my dormer window
A pot geranium flies its bright balloon,
Nor can the festering hot-house of the tropics
Breed a tenser crimson, for this crock of soil,
Six inches deep by four across,
Contains the pattern, the prod and pulse of life,
Complete as the Nile or the Niger.
                              And what need therefore
To stretch for the straining kite? – for kite and flower
Bloom in my room for ever; the light that lifts them
Shines in my own eyes, and my body's warmth
Hatches their red in my veins. It is the Gulf Stream
That rains down the chimney, making the soot spit; it is
   the Trade Wind

That blows in the draught under the bedroom door.
My ways are circumscribed, confined as a limpet
To one small radius of rock; yet
I eat the equator, breathe the sky, and carry
The great white sun in the dirt of my finger-nails.

Norman Nicholson

STRANGE MEETING

It seemed that out of battle I escaped
Down some profound dull tunnel, long since scooped
Through granites which titanic wars had groined.
Yet also there encumbered sleepers groaned,
Too fast in thought or death to be bestirred.
Then, as I probed them, one sprang up, and stared
With piteous recognition in fixed eyes,
Lifting distressful hands as if to bless.
And by his smile, I knew that sullen hall,
By his dead smile I knew we stood in Hell.
With a thousand pains that vision's face was grained;
Yet no blood reached there from the upper ground,
And no guns thumped, or down the flues made moan.
'Strange friend,' I said, 'here is no cause to mourn.'
'None,' said the other, 'save the undone years,
The hopelessness. Whatever hope is yours,
Was my life also; I went hunting wild
After the wildest beauty in the world,
Which lies not calm in eyes, or braided hair,
But mocks the steady running of the hour,
And if it grieves, grieves richlier than here.
For by my glee might many men have laughed,
And of my weeping something had been left,
Which must die now. I mean the truth untold,
The pity of war, the pity war distilled.
Now men will go content with what we spoiled.
Or, discontent, boil bloody, and be spilled.
They will be swift with swiftness of the tigress,
None will break ranks, though nations trek from
    progress.

Courage was mine, and I had mystery,
Wisdom was mine, and I had mastery;
To miss the march of this retreating world
Into vain citadels that are not walled.
Then, when much blood had clogged their
    chariot-wheels
I would go up and wash them from sweet wells,
Even with truths that lie too deep for taint.
I would have poured my spirit without stint
But not through wounds; not on the cess of war.
Foreheads of men have bled where no wounds were.
I am the enemy you killed, my friend.
I knew you in this dark; for so you frowned
Yesterday through me as you jabbed and killed.
I parried; but my hands were loath and cold.
Let us sleep now . . .'

Wilfred Owen

SCHOOLMISTRESS – MISS HUMM

Straight-backed as a Windsor chair
She stood on the top playground step
And surveyed her Saturnalian kingdom.
At 8.45 precisely, she stiffened
(If that were possible), produced a key
– A large, cold dungeon-key –
Placed it below her lip, and blew.
No summons from Heaven itself
(It was a church school) was more imperious!
No angel trumpet or Mosean thunder-clap
Calling the Israelites to doom or repentance
Met swifter obedience. No Gorgon
Suspended life with such efficiency.
In the middle of a shout, a scream,
We halted. Our faces froze.
No longer George or Tom or Mary,
But forty reproductions of a single child,
Chilled to conformity. We gathered
Like captive troops and, climbing steps,

Received the inspection of her cool eyes,
Willing them away from unwashed necks
Or black-ringed fingernails,
But knowing our very thoughts were visible
If she chose to see. Nothing escaped her.
She was (as I said, a church school)
God, St Michael, the Recording Angel
And, in our guiltier moments, Lucifer –
A Lucifer in long tweed skirts
And a blouse severely fastened at the neck
By a round cameo that was no ornament
But the outward sign of inward authority.
Even the Rector, when he stepped inside
And the brown walls rumbled to his voice,
Dwindled to a curate . . .
It would have astonished us to learn, I think,
That she ate supper, went to bed,
And even, perhaps, on occasions, slept.

Clive Sansom

SONG OF SOLOMON

I am the rose of Sharon, and the lily of the valleys. As the lily
among thorns, so is my love among the daughters. As the
apple tree among the trees of the wood, so is my beloved
among the sons. I sat down under his shadow with great
delight, and his fruit was sweet to my taste. He brought me
to the banqueting house, and his banner over me was love.
Stay me with flagons, comfort me with apples: for I am sick
of love. His left hand is under my head, and his right hand
doth embrace me. I charge you, O ye daughters of Jerusalem, by the roes, and by the hinds of the field, that ye stir
not up, nor awake my love, till he please. The voice of my
beloved! behold, he cometh leaping upon the mountains,
skipping upon the hills. My beloved is like a roe or a young
hart: behold, he standeth behind our wall, he looketh forth
at the windows, shewing himself through the lattice. My
beloved spake, and said unto me, Rise up, my love, my fair
one, and come away. For, lo, the winter in past, the rain is

over and gone; The flowers appear on the earth; the time of
the singing of birds is come, and the voice of the turtle is
heard in our land; The fig tree putteth forth her green figs,
and the vines with the tender grape give a good smell. Arise,
my love, my fair one, and come away.

THE THIRTY-NINE STEPS

I was in a wide semicircle of moorland, with the brown river
as radius, and the high hills forming the northern circumfer-
ence. There was not a sign or sound of a human being, only
the plashing water and the interminable crying of curlews.
Yet, oddly enough, for the first time I felt the terror of the
hunted on me. It was not the police that I thought of, but the
other folk, who knew that I knew Scudder's secret and dared
not let me live. I was certain that they would pursue me with
a keenness and vigilance unknown to the British law, and
that once their grip closed on me I should find no mercy.

I looked back, but there was nothing in the landscape. The
sun glinted on the metals of the line and the wet stones in the
stream, and you could not have found a more peaceful sight
in the world. Nevertheless I started to run. Crouching low in
the runnels of the bog, I ran till the sweat blinded my eyes.
The mood did not leave me till I had reached the rim of
mountain and flung myself panting on a ridge high above the
young waters of the brown river.

From my vantage-ground I could scan the whole moor
right away to the railway line and to the south of it where
green fields took the place of heather. I have eyes like a
hawk, but I could see nothing moving in the whole countryside. Then I looked east beyond the ridge and saw a new
kind of landscape – shallow green valleys with plentiful fir
plantations and the faint lines of dust which spoke of
highroads. Last of all I looked into the blue May sky, and
there I saw that which set my pulses racing . . .

Low down in the south a monoplane was climbing into
the heavens. I was as certain as if I had been told that that
aeroplane was looking for me, and that it did not belong to
the police. For an hour or two I watched it from a pit of
heather. It flew low along the hilltops, and then in narrow

circles over the valley up which I had come. Then it seemed to change its mind, rose to a great height, and flew away back to the south.

I did not like this espionage from the air, and I began to think less well of the countryside I had chosen for a refuge. These heather hills were no sort of cover if my enemies were in the sky, and I must find a different kind of sanctuary. I looked with more satisfaction to the green country beyond the ridge, for there I should find woods and stone houses.

About six in the evening I came out of the moorland to a white ribbon of road which wound up the narrow vale of a lowland stream. As I followed it, fields gave place to bent, the glen became a plateau, and presently I had reached a kind of pass where a solitary house smoked in the twilight. The road swung over a bridge, and leaning on the parapet was a young man.

John Buchan

THE DIARY OF FANNY BURNEY

The Queen made Mrs Delaney sit next her, and Miss Port brought her some tea.

The King, meanwhile, came to me again, and said: 'Are you musical?'

'Not a performer, sir.'

Then, going from me to the Queen, he cried: 'She does not play.'

I did not hear what the Queen answered; she spoke in a low voice and seemed much out of spirits.

The King returned to me, and said:

'Are you sure you never play? Never touch the keys at all?'

'Never to acknowledge it, sir.'

'Oh! that's it!' cried he; and flying to the Queen, cried: 'She does play – but not to acknowledge it!'

The eager air with which he returned to me fully explained what was to follow. I hastily, therefore, spoke first, in order to stop him, crying: 'I never, sir, played to anybody but myself! Never!'

'No? Are you sure?' cried he, disappointed; 'but – but you'll . . .'

'I have never, sir,' cried I, very earnestly, 'played in my life, but when I could hear nobody else – quite alone, and from a mere love of musical sounds.'

There ensued a long silence, and we drank tea.

Sometime afterwards, the King said he found by the newspapers that Mrs Clive was dead. This led on to the players, and thence to Mrs Siddons.

'I am an enthusiast for her,' cried the King, 'quite an enthusiast. I think there was never any player in my time so excellent – not Garrick himself; I own it!'

Then, coming close to me, who was silent, he said:

'What? What?' – meaning what say you? But I still said nothing.

From players he went to plays, and complained of the great want of good modern comedies, and of the extreme immorality of most of the old ones, till at last he came to Shakespeare.

'Was there ever,' cried he, 'such stuff as great part of Shakespeare? only one must not say so! But what think you? – What? – Is there not sad stuff? What? – what?'

'Yes, indeed, I think so, sir, though mixed with such excellences that –'

'Oh!' cried he, 'I know it is not to be said! but it's true. Only it's Shakespeare, and nobody dare abuse him.'

Fanny Burney

JAMAICA INN

The light of her candle played upon the walls, but it did not reach to the top of the stairs, where the darkness gaped at her like a gulf.

She knew she could never climb those stairs again, nor tread that empty landing. Whatever lay beyond her and above must rest there undisturbed. Death had come upon the house to-night, and its brooding spirit still hovered in the air. She felt now that this was what Jamaica Inn had always waited for and feared. The damp walls, the creaking boards, the whispers in the air, and the footsteps that had no name: these were the warning of a house that had felt itself long threatened.

Mary shivered; and she knew that the quality of this silence had origin in far-off buried and forgotten things.

She dreaded panic, above all things; the scream that forced itself to the lips, the wild stumble of groping feet and hands that beat the air for passage. She was afraid that it might come to her, destroying reason; and, now that the first shock of discovery had lessened, she knew that it might force its way upon her, close in and stifle her. Her fingers might lose their sense of grip and touch, and the candle fall from her hands. Then she would be alone, and covered by the darkness. The tearing desire to run seized hold of her, and she conquered it. She backed away from the hall towards the passage, the candle flickering in the draught of air, and when she came to the kitchen and saw the door still open to the patch of garden, her calm deserted her, and she ran blindly through the door to the cold free air outside, a sob in her throat, her outstretched hands grazing the stone wall as she turned the corner of the house. She ran like a thing pursued across the yard, and came to the open road, where the familiar stalwart figure of the squire's groom confronted her. He put out his hands to save her, and she groped at his belt, feeling for security, her teeth chattering now in the full shock of reaction.

'He's dead,' she said; 'he's dead there on the floor. I saw him'; and, try as she did, she could not stop this chattering of her teeth and the shivering of her body. He led her to the side of the road, back to the trap, and he reached for the cloak and put it around her, and she held it to her close, grateful for the warmth.

'He's dead,' she repeated; 'stabbed in the back; I saw the place where his coat was rent, and there was blood. He lay on his face. The clock had fallen with him. The blood was dry; and he looked as though he had lain there for some time. The inn was dark and silent. No one else was there.'

'Was your aunt gone?' whispered the man.

Mary shook her head. 'I don't know. I did not see. I had to come away.'

He saw by her face that her strength had gone, and she

would fall, and he helped her up into the trap and climbed on to the seat beside her.

'All right, then,' he said, 'all right. Sit quiet, then, here. No one shall hurt you. There now. All right, then.' His gruff voice helped her, and she crouched beside him in the trap, the warm cloak muffled to her chin.

'That was no sight for a maid to see,' he told her. 'You should have let me go. I wish now you'd have stayed back here in the trap. That's terrible for you to see him lying dead there, murdered.'

Talking eased her, and his rough sympathy was good. 'The pony was still in the stable,' she said. 'I listened at the door and heard him move. They had never even finished their preparations for going. The kitchen door was unlocked and there were bundles on the floor there; blankets too, ready to load into the cart. It must have happened several hours ago.'

'It puzzles me what the squire is doing,' said Richards. 'He should have been here before this. I'd feel easier if he'd come, and you could tell your story to him. There's been bad work here to-night. You should never have come.'

Daphne du Maurier

THE HEART OF THE MATTER

As soon as he heard the door close, he took out the cigarette carton in which he kept the ten doses of Evipan. He added two more doses for greater certainty – to have exceeded by two doses in ten days could not, surely, be regarded as suspicious. After that he took a long drink of whisky and sat still and waited for courage with the tablets in the palm of his hand. Now, he thought, I am absolutely alone: this was freezing-point.

But he was wrong, Solitude itself has a voice. It said to him, Throw away those tablets. You'll never be able to collect enough again. You'll be saved. Give up play-acting. Mount the stairs to bed and have a good night's sleep. In the morning you'll be woken by your boy, and you'll drive down to the police station for a day's ordinary work. The voice dwelt on the word 'ordinary' as it might have dwelt on the word 'happy' or 'peaceful'.

'No,' Scobie said aloud, 'no.' He pushed the tablets in his mouth six at a time, and drank them down in two draughts. Then he opened his diary and wrote against November 12, *Called on H.R., out; temperature at 2 p.m.* and broke abruptly off as though at that moment he had been gripped by the final pain. Afterwards he sat bolt upright and waited what seemed a long while for any indication at all of approaching death; he had no idea how it would come to him. He tried to pray, but the Hail Mary evaded his memory, and he was aware of his heartbeats like a clock striking the hour. He tried out an act of contrition, but when he reached, 'I am sorry and beg pardon', a cloud formed over the door and drifted down over the whole room and he couldn't remember what it was that he had to be sorry for. He had to hold himself upright with both hands, but he had forgotten the reason why he so held himself. Somewhere far away he thought he heard the sounds of pain. 'A storm,' he said aloud, 'there's going to be a storm,' as the clouds grew, and he tried to get up to close the windows. 'Ali,' he called, 'Ali.' It seemed to him as though someone outside the room were seeking him, calling him, and he made a last effort to indicate that he was here. He got to his feet and heard the hammer of his heart beating out a reply. He had a message to convey, but the darkness and the storm drove it back within the case of his breast, and all the time outside the house, outside the world that drummed like hammer blows within his ear, someone wandered, seeking to get in, someone appealing for help, someone in need of him. And automatically at the call of need, at the cry of a victim, Scobie strung himself to act. He dredged his consciousness up from an infinite distance in order to make some reply. He said aloud, 'Dear God, I love . . .' but the effort was too great and he did not feel his body when it struck the floor or hear the small tinkle of the medal as it span like a coin under the ice-box – the saint whose name nobody could remember.

Graham Greene

The water looked damp and chilly; the wind felt cold.

'Well, who's going to be first in?' said Harris at last.

There was no rush for precedence. George settled the matter so far as he was concerned by retiring into the boat and pulling on his socks. Montmorency gave vent to an involuntary howl, as if merely thinking of the thing had given him the horrors; and Harris said it would be so difficult to get into the boat again, and went back and sorted out his trousers.

I did not altogether like to give in, though I did not relish the plunge. There might be snags about, or weeds, I thought. I meant to compromise matters by going down to the edge and just throwing the water over myself; so I took a towel and crept out on the bank and wormed my way along on to the branch of a tree that dipped down into the water.

It was bitterly cold. The wind cut like a knife. I thought I would not throw the water over myself after all. I would go back into the boat and dress; and I turned to do so; and, as I turned, the silly branch gave way, and I and the towel went in together with a tremendous splash, and I was out mid-stream with a gallon of Thames water inside me before I knew what had happened.

'By Jove! old J.'s gone in,' I heard Harris say, as I came blowing to the surface. 'I didn't think he'd have the pluck to do it. Did you?'

'Is it all right?' sang out George.

'Lovely,' I spluttered back. 'You are duffers not to come in. I wouldn't have missed this for worlds. Why don't you try it? It only wants a little determination.'

But I could not persuade them.

Rather an amusing thing happened while dressing that morning. I was very cold when I got back into the boat, and, in my hurry to get my shirt on, I accidentally jerked it into the water. It made me awfully wild, especially as George burst out laughing. I could not see anything to laugh at, and I told George so, and he only laughed the more. I never saw a man laugh so much. I quite lost my temper with him at last, and I pointed out to him what a drivelling maniac of an imbecile idiot he was; but he only roared the louder. And then, just as I was landing the shirt, I noticed that it was not my shirt at all, but George's, which I had mistaken for mine; whereupon the humour of the thing struck me for the first time, and *I* began to laugh. And the more I looked from George's wet shirt to George, roaring with laughter, the more I was amused, and I laughed so much that I had to let the shirt fall back into the water again.

'Ar'n't you – you – going to get it out?' said George between his shrieks.

I could not answer him at all for a while, I was laughing so, but at last, between my peals I managed to jerk out:

'It isn't my shirt – it's *yours*!'

I never saw a man's face change from lively to severe so suddenly in all my life before.

'What!' he yelled, springing up. 'You silly cuckoo! Why can't you be more careful what you're doing? Why the deuce don't you go and dress on the bank? You're not fit to be in a boat, you're not. Gimme the hitcher.'

I tried to make him see the fun of the thing, but he could not. George is very dense at seeing a joke sometimes.

Jerome K. Jerome

CRY THE BELOVED COUNTRY

There is a lovely road that runs from Ixopo into the hills. These hills are grass-covered and rolling, and they are lovely beyond any singing of it. The road climbs seven miles into them, to Carisbrooke; and from there, if there is no mist, you look down on one of the fairest valleys of Africa. About you there is grass and bracken and you may hear the forlorn crying of the titihoya, one of the birds of the veld. Below you is the valley of the Umzimkulu, on its journey from the Drakensberg to the sea; and beyond and behind the river, great hill after great hill; and beyond and behind them, the mountains of Ingeli and East Griqualand.

The grass is rich and matted, you cannot see the soil. It holds the rain and the mist, and they seep into the ground, feeding the streams in every kloof. It is well-tended, and not too many cattle feed upon it; not too many fires burn it, laying bare the soil. Stand unshod upon it, for the ground is holy, being even as it came from the Creator. Keep it, guard it, care for it, for it keeps men, guards men, cares for men. Destroy it and man is destroyed.

Where you stand the grass is rich and matted, you cannot see the soil. But the rich green hills break down. They fall to the valley below, and falling, change their nature. For they grow red and bare; they cannot hold the rain and mist, and the streams are dry in the kloofs. Too many cattle feed upon the grass, and too many fires have burned it. Stand shod upon it, for it is coarse and sharp, and the stones cut under the feet. It is not kept, or guarded, or cared for, it no longer keeps men, guards men, cares for men. The titihoya does not cry here any more.

The great red hills stand desolate, and the earth has torn away like flesh. The lightning flashes over them, the clouds pour down upon them, the dead streams come to life, full of the red blood of the earth. Down in the valleys women scratch the soil that is left, and the maize hardly reaches the height of a man. They are valleys of old men and old women, of mothers and children. The men are away, the young men and the girls are away. The soil cannot keep them any more.

Alan Paton

A PROSPECT OF THE SEA

And she, alone in the house, was sewing her new dress. It was a bright country dress with flowers on the bodice. Only a few more stitches were needed before it would be ready to wear. It would lie neat on her shoulders, and two of the flowers would be growing out of her breasts.

When she walked with her husband on Sunday mornings over the fields and down into the village, the boys would smile at her behind their hands, and the shaping of the dress round her belly would set all the widow women talking. She slipped into her new dress, and, looking into the mirror over the fire-place, saw that it was prettier than she had imagined. It made her face paler and her long hair darker. She had cut it low.

149

A dog out in the night lifted its head up and howled. She turned away hurriedly from her reflection, and pulled the curtains closer.

Out in the night they were searching for a madman. He had green eyes, they said, and had married a lady. They said he had cut off her lips because she smiled at men. They took him away, but he stole a knife from the kitchen and slashed his keeper and broke out into the wild valleys.

From afar he saw the light in the house, and stumbled up to the edge of the garden. He felt, he did not see, the little fence around it. The rusting wire scraped on his hands, and the wet, abominable grass crept over his knees. And once he was through the fence, the hosts of the garden came rushing to meet him, the flower-headed, and the bodying frosts. He had torn his fingers while the old wounds were still wet. Like a man of blood he came out of the enemy's darkness on to the steps. He said in a whisper: 'Let them not shoot me.' And he opened the door.

She was in the middle of the room. Her hair had fallen untidily, and three of the buttons at the neck of her dress were undone. What made the dog howl as it did? Frightened of the howling, and thinking of the tales she had heard, she rocked in her chair. What became of the woman? she wondered as she rocked. She could not think of a woman without any lips. What became of women without any lips? she wondered.

The door made no noise. He stepped into the room, trying to smile, and holding out his hands.

'Oh, you've come back,' she said.

Then she turned in her chair and saw him. There was blood even by his green eyes. She put her fingers to her mouth. 'Not shoot,' he said.

But the moving of her arm drew the neck of her dress apart, and he stared in wonder at her wide, white forehead, her frightened eyes and mouth, and down on to the flowers on her dress. With the moving of her arm, her dress danced in the light. She sat before him, covered in flowers. 'Sleep,' said the madman. And kneeling down, he put his bewildered head upon her lap.

Dylan Thomas

ACKNOWLEDGMENTS

For permission to reprint the copyright material in this anthology we make grateful acknowledgment to the following authors, publishers and executors:

Aitken and Stone for *Thomasina* by Paul Gallico; Allen and Unwin for *You'd Better Believe Him* by Brian Patten, and *All Day It has Rained* by Alun Lewis; A. and C. Black for *The Dustman* by Clive Sansom; Blackie for *The Silver Road* by Hamish Hendry, and *As Fit As A Fiddle* by Pauline Clarke; Bloodaxe Books for *The Scholar Speaks, In Her Retirement* by John Cassidy (from *Nightcries*); Breakwater Books for *Roger Was A Razor Fish* by Al Pitman; Burns and Oates for *Worzel Gummidge* by Barbara Euphan Todd; Sylvia Bryant for *Shopping* by Mary Williams; Jonathan Cape for *Emil And The Detectives* by Erich Kästner, translated by Eileen Hall, *Cry The Beloved Country* by Alan Paton, *The Lesson* and *He Who Owns The Whistle, Rules The World* by Roger McGough, and *The BFG* by Roald Dahl and the illustrator Quentin Blake; Jonathan Cape and the executors of the estate of C. Day Lewis for *The Album* by C. Day Lewis; Jonathan Cape and the estate of Robert Frost for *Stopping By Woods On A Snowy Evening* by Robert Frost; Jonathan Cape and the estate of Teresa Hooley for *Christmas* by Teresa Hooley; Jonathan Cape and the estate of Arthur Ransome for *Swallowdale* by Arthur Ransome; Laura Cecil and the estate of James Reeves for *The Grey Horse* and *The Wind* by James Reeves; Century Hutchinson for *Help!* by Barbara Ireson, and *The Art of Coarse Acting* by Michael Green; Chatto and Windus and the estate of Daisy Ashford for *The Young Visiters* by Daisy Ashford; Chatto and Windus and the estate of Sylvia Townsend Warner for *Mr Fortune's Maggot* by Sylvia Townsend Warner; Chatto and Windus and the estate of Virginia Woolf for *Duchess And The Jeweller* and *To The Lighthouse*; Marchette Chute for *Undersea* by Marchette Chute (originally published in *Child Life* magazine); William Collins for *Paddington Abroad* by Michael Bond, and *The Lion, The Witch And The Wardrobe* by C. S. Lewis, © C. S. Lewis Pte Ltd; Curtis Brown for *Jamaica Inn* by Daphne du Maurier, and *Between Birthdays* by Ogden Nash; Paul Dehn Enterprises for *Exercise Book* by Paul Dehn; André Deutsch for *The Germ* and *The People Upstairs* by Ogden Nash, *I Can't Stay Long* and *Christmas Landscape* by Laurie Lee, and *I'm The Big Sleeper* by Michael Rosen; Mary Jeffries for *Late For Breakfast* by Mary Dawson; Dobson Books for *Who?* by Leonard Clark; Gerald Duckworth for *The Llama* and *The Microbe* by Hilaire Belloc; Faber and Faber for *Musée Des Beaux Arts* and '*Stop All The Clocks, Cut Off The Telephone*' by W. H. Auden (from *Collected Poems*), *The Pot Geranium* by Norman Nicholson, *Blackberry Picking, Trout* and *Digging* by Seamus Heaney (from *Death Of A Naturalist*), *Gus, The Theatre Cat* by T. S. Eliot (from *Old Possum's Book Of Practical Cats*), *Good Dreams* by Louis

MacNeice (from *Collected Poems*), *The Iron Man* and *How The Cat Became* by Ted Hughes (from *The Iron Man and How The Whale Became and Other Stories*), and *Mr Bleaney* by Philip Larkin (from *The Whitsun Weddings*); Samuel French and George Harrap for *The Diary Of Fanny Burney* (from *The Hollow Crown* devised by John Barton); Victor Gollancz for *My Cousin Rachel* by Daphne du Maurier, *Hatter's Castle* by A. J. Cronin, and *I Am The Cheese* by Robert Cormier; Granada Publishing for *Maggie And Milly And Molly And May* by e. e. cummings (from *Complete Poems 1913–62*); Graham Greene for *Monsignor Quixote* by Graham Greene; George Harrap for *Anne Of Green Gables* by L. M. Montgomery; A. M. Heath and Jonathan Cape for *Saville* by David Storey; William Heinemann for *General Store* by Rachel Field, *Dear Me* by Peter Ustinov, and *Of Mice And Men* by John Steinbeck; David Higham for *Billy Liar* by Keith Waterhouse, *Let Sleeping Vets Lie* by James Herriot, *Who* and *Timothy Winters* by Charles Causley, *The Enemies* by Elizabeth Jennings, *A Prospect Of The Sea* by Dylan Thomas, *Staying On* by Paul Scott, and *The New Year* by Ted Walker; Houghton Mifflin for *The Wizard Of Earthsea* by Ursula K. LeGuin; Michael Joseph for *A Quiet Year* by Derek Tangye; Little, Brown for *Eletelephony* by Laura E. Richards (from *Tirra Lirra: Rymes Old and New*); Edward Lowbury for *Prince Kano* by Edward Lowbury (from *Green Magic*); James MacGibbon, executor, for *My Hat* by Stevie Smith (from *Collected Poems*); Macmillan for *Just William* by Richmal Crompton, *Chameleon* by Alan Brownjohn (from *Brownjohn's Beasts*); Macmillan Publishing Company (New York) for *The famous Human Cannonball* by Jack Prelutsky (from *Circus!*); Methuen for *The Enchanted Places* by Christopher Milne; Macdonald for *Flight Of The Roller-Coaster* by Raymond Souster (from *Delights And Warnings*); John Murray for *Diary Of A Church Mouse* and *Executive* by John Betjeman (from *Collected Poems*); James Kirkup for *Earthquake* by James Kirkup; Oxford University Press for *Lark Rise To Candleford* by Flora Thompson, and *Pippi Longstocking* by Astrid Lindgren, translated by Edna Hurup; Penguin Books for *Ring Of Bright Water* by Gavin Maxwell, *A Boy's Head* by Miroslav Holub, translated by Ian Milner and George Theiner (from *Selected Poems*), and *The Song Of The Whale* by Kit Wright (from *Hot Dog and Other Poems*); Mrs D. Peters for *Under The Stairs* by Daphne Lister; Laurence Pollinger for *The Heart Of The Matter* by Graham Greene; Laurence Pollinger and estate of Frieda Lawrence Ravagli for *The Piano* by D. H. Lawrence; Martin Secker and Warburg for *In Moonlight* by Andrew Young (from *The Poetical Works of Andrew Young*); Anthony Sheil for *The French Lieutenant's Woman* by John Fowles, and *A Poet In The Family* by Dannie Abse; The Society of Authors for *Dear Sir, Drop Dead* by Bernard Shaw; The Society of Authors on behalf of Mrs Iris Wise for *The Shell* by James Stephens; the literary trustees of Walter de la Mare and the Society of Authors as their representative for *The Old Summerhouse, Snow, Five Eyes* and *John Mouldy* by Walter de la Mare; the Society of Authors as the literary representative of the estate of Rose Fyleman for *Witch, Witch*; Virago for *Me Again* by Stevie Smith; A. P. Watt, Macmillan and M. B. Yeats for *When You Are Old* by W. B. Yeats (from *Collected Poems*); A. P. Watt, as the executors of the estate of Robert Graves, for *The Pumpkin* by Robert Graves (from *Collected Poems*); A. P. Watt, as the trustees of the Wodehouse Trust No. 3, and Century Hutchinson for *Summer Lightning* by P. G. Wodehouse; A. P. Watt, on behalf of the executors of the estate of Robert Graves, for *Warning To Children* by Robert Graves (from *Collected Poems*); A. P. Watt, on behalf of The Rt. Hon. Lord Tweedsmuir CBE, for *The Thirty-Nine Steps* by John Buchan.

Every effort has been made to trace the owners of copyright material but difficulties have arisen in a few cases of contested or transferred ownership. We apologise to anyone whom our enquiries did not reach and we invite them to apply to LAMDA for proper acknowledgment.

INDEX OF AUTHORS

INDEX OF TITLES